Native Americans

James Lagomarsino

Published by TAJ Books International LLC 2013

219 Great Lake Drive, Cary,
NC 27519
USA

www.tajbooks.com

The publishers would like to thank the following contributors for the use of their photography:
Shutterstock, Mike Loiselle, Miro Vrlik Photography, Radoslaw Lecyk, Knumina Studios,
Spirit of America, Digital Media Pro, Josef Hanus, cdrin., Leoboudv, ppart, Cura Photography, Miro Vrlik Photography, Carptrash,
Laslovarga Heironymous Rowe, Herb Roe

ISBN-13: 978-1-84406-316-1

Printed in China.

1 2 3 4 5 17 16 15 14 13

CONTENTS

INTRODUCTION

The history of the American native peoples is a long and fascinating one. The issues of who they are and where they came from have become the center of attention for many studies. From simple enthusiasts to learned scholars, people have spent anything from hours to years trying to find out more about the subject. Young and old alike are caught by the allure of Native Americans and their cultures. There are so many different aspects—from folklore to hunting skills—that surely something wonderful can be learned by everyone who shows an interest.

Sadly, the full story of the native peoples will never be known as many vital facts have been lost in the mists of time. Many cultures became extinct through disease or warfare well before the arrival of European settlers.

Many different theories exist as to where the Native American peoples came from, as well as exactly how they made the journey. The most widely accepted hypothesis is that they traveled from Asia into Alaska via Russia. Today the two continents are separated by a shallow sea known as the Bering Sound. During the last ice-age, approximately 20,000–30,000 years ago, the falling sea levels formed a land-bridge that stretched from northeastern Siberia into Alaska, thus making it possible to cross from continent to continent on foot. Other theories suggest that the first settlers actually arrived on boats across the sea rather than by land. If this was the case, the most likely routes would be from Polynesia across the Pacific Ocean, or from Scandinavia across the northern Atlantic Ocean. It is possible that the ancestral Americans came via both methods.

A third theory is that the natives were always there from the start. Although no physical evidence supports this theory, many tribal cultures have legends which state that they were created in their homelands at the beginning of time.

It is likely that the land bridge was uncovered and recovered by the changing sea levels many times during the last ice-age. If this was the case, it would account for the fact that there were probably several different waves of migration. The common physical features demonstrated by the many different tribes or nations of Native Americans indicate that they have the same origin. The many different languages spoken by them, however, would suggest that they arrived at different times. If there were several distinct migrations, it would help to explain the linguistic variations and complexity seen today.

As each wave of migration across the land bridge occurred, the new immigrants spread out from Alaska, going east and south into Canada and beyond. The popular view is that at least three separate migration waves occurred on the basis of a mixture of archaeological and anthropological evidence. Since then, however, population genetics has shown that there were four major periods of migration, with many smaller events in between. The vast majority of the migrants were from Asia, although genetic evidence seems to suggest that at least some of them came from Europe.

It is generally accepted that the first wave, which constituted the oldest Indian cultures in North America, was led by the Sandia peoples. Others believe, however, that the Sandia peoples were pre-dated by as much as 10,000 years by earlier civilizations.

The Sandia culture existed around 15000 BC, and about three thousand years later, around 12000 BC, the Clovis people made their appearance. During this era, known as the late Pleistocene epoch, large mammals, such as woolly mammoths and giant sloths, provided good hunting for the early settlers. By the time the Folsom culture developed around 8000 BC, most of these massive creatures had died out. Just how much being hunted by humans contributed to their demise is a subject of hot debate among scientists today. The Folsom peoples were primarily bison hunters.

The second wave was composed of the Athabascan peoples, the early ancestors of many of today's better-known tribes, such as the Navajos and Apaches. The third and last major immigration wave included the Inuits, Yuits, and Aleuts. Because the world's sea levels had risen considerably since well before the third wave of migrants arrived, the Bering land bridge was not

was not the means by which they traveled to North America. Whether they crossed by boat is not known, but many of them were skilled in the use of the kayak so it is highly likely. These later arrivals were so different from those of the two earlier migration waves that they are often classed separately. As a result they are not normally considered to be included in the term "Native American Indians."

It was not long before the migrating peoples had established thriving cultures. These fell into seven basic geographic regions north of Mexico: Arctic and Sub-Arctic, Northwest Coast, Plains and Prairie, Plateau and Great Basin, Northeast, Southwest, and Southeast.

When Christopher Columbus arrived in 1492 the continent was sparsely populated. Some say that there were as many as 10 million people living north of Mexico, although it is likely that the figure was closer to 2 million. Either way, for such a big land mass, this was a small population. Unfortunately, the Spanish explorers and the European settlers that followed brought with them dreadful diseases such as smallpox, chicken pox, influenza, and measles. Because the Native American peoples had not been exposed to these virulent sicknesses before and thus had developed no immunity against them, these diseases had a catastrophic effect on their populations. Within the first hundred years of contact with Europeans, tens of thousands died as a result of disease. Some estimates suggest that more than 80% of certain Native American populations died in these terrible times.

When Christopher Columbus first reached the shores of America, he was actually looking for the East Indies. Believing that he had found them, he called the natives "Indians." This name stuck, although there are many variations on the term. Alternatives include Amerindians, Amerins, Indyans, Injuns, or Red Indians. It is a controversial subject, and as political attitudes change, so the "correct" terminology varies. The most popular names in the United States are currently "Native Americans" or "American Indians." In Canada, the term "First Nations" is commonly used, whereas in Alaska the preference is "Alaskan Natives," to take into account the presence of Inuit, Yupik, and Aleut peoples.

Although many of the native tribes were friendly to the European explorers, the first group that Columbus met were the Arawaks on Haiti. Most of the 250,000 members of the tribe were violently enslaved by the Europeans and within 100 years only 500 remained. Within a few decades, the entire culture was extinct. Whereas this is the most drastic example of native cultures being eradicated by European behavior, over the next 400 years many other native cultures in the Americas suffered at the hands of Europeans.

One of the biggest areas of conflict between the Native American peoples and the European settlers concerned the interactions of man and nature. For many of the indigenous tribes, achieving harmony with the natural and spiritual worlds was of prime importance. This contrasted strongly with the approach the Europeans took, who viewed all they saw as an infinite resource for exploitation. For example, they believed a limitless supply of animals existed that could be killed for meat or to generate profits from fur trading and that the endless forests were available to be cut down to provide timber or firewood. In some ways the belief that these resources were infinite is understandable because to the Europeans the sheer scale of the country must have been overwhelming. The concept that the natural bounty around them could not take sustained exploitation was beyond their understanding.

Many native peoples found the European settlers' abuse of the environment to be unforgivable. In addition, the European habit of claiming title to the ownership of lands that were historically those of native tribes created major conflicts. Some of the disconnect arose because settlers generally considered the natives to be nomadic and therefore not interested in land ownership.

As more and more Europeans arrived, the pressure for living space grew. It was not long before tribes were being displaced, and this often ended in physical confrontation. The Indian Wars were met with absolute resolve by the white government, who put massive military forces into troubled areas to quell any

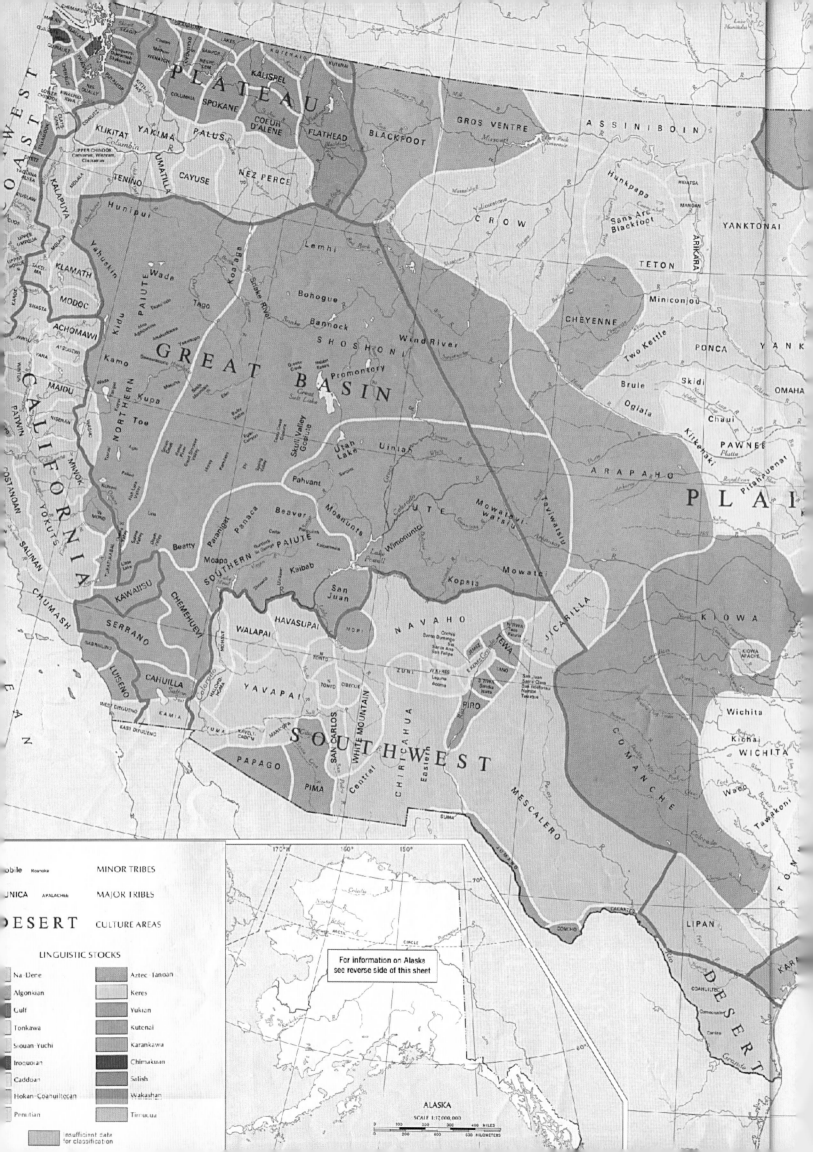

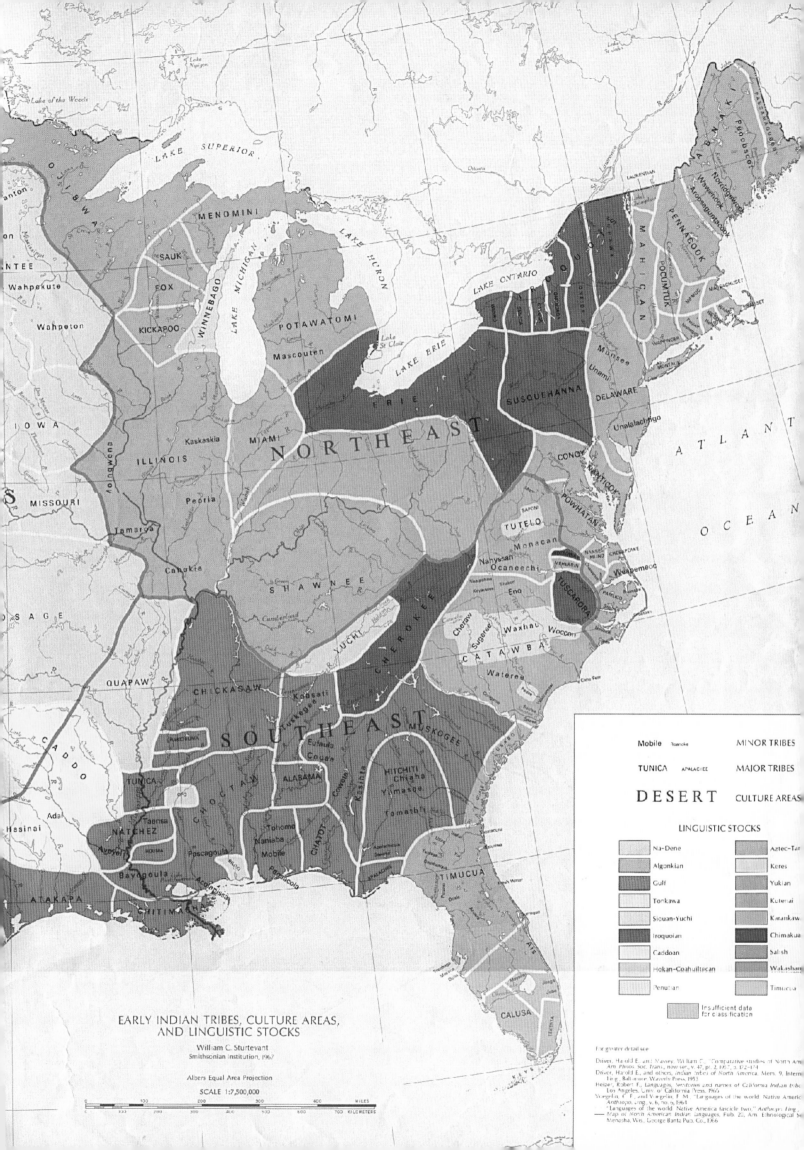

EARLY INDIAN TRIBES, CULTURE AREAS,
AND LINGUISTIC STOCKS

William C. Sturtevant
Smithsonian Institution, 1967

Albers Equal Area Projection

SCALE 1:7,500,000

Mobile	Roanoke	MINOR TRIBES
TUNICA	APALACHEE	MAJOR TRIBES
DESERT		CULTURE AREAS

LINGUISTIC STOCKS

- Na-Dene
- Algonkian
- Gulf
- Tonkawa
- Siouan-Yuchi
- Iroquoian
- Caddoan
- Hokan-Coahuiltecan
- Penutian
- Aztec-Tan
- Keres
- Yukian
- Kutenai
- Karankawa
- Chimakua
- Salish
- Wakashan
- Timucua

Insufficient data
for classification

uprisings. Often the authorities would make treaties to gain some form of peace, then would ignore or nullify them, leaving the Native Americans high and dry.

On January 31, 1876, the United States government finally ordered all Native Americans to move from their homelands onto reservations or reserves. Many tribal factions refused to comply, and a series of battles ensued. The Native Americans were doomed to lose in the end, however, because they were outnumbered, outgunned, and unable to unite against the enemy. One of the last, and in many ways most famous, clashes occurred in 1890, when the U.S. cavalry massacred large numbers of Indian warriors, along with defenceless women and children at Wounded Knee in South Dakota.

The story of the arrival of European settlers is not all bad, however. The Americas had been without horses since the end of the Ice Age, forcing Native Americans to travel across land on foot. Hunting bison was a very difficult and unproductive affair unless the hunter could keep pace with them. Thus, when settlers brought horses with them, it was not long before the Native Americans obtained their own. Some of these were undoubtedly stolen, others were captured horses bred in the wild. But once they had their own horses, the culture of many tribes changed overnight. They were able to chase bison over large distances, and after making their kills, they were able to transport the carcasses home with ease. This led to a level of prosperity many had never experienced before. Although it was a time of plenty, the Native Americans understood the importance of remaining in balance with nature. As a result of this they only took what they could use. This was in stark contrast to the Europeans who would often kill huge numbers of bison just for their tongues, which were considered a delicacy. The remaining animal carcasses were just left to rot, something that was perceived as a crime against nature by Native Americans.

After the Indian Wars were over, various methods were used to try and "civilize" the Native Americans. Some of these practices imposed untold misery on the unfortunate subjects. For over 50 years, from 1875 to 1928, children were forcibly taken from their tribal homes and sent to boarding schools where they were forbidden to speak their own languages and forced

to speak English instead as well as follow European religions. Other indignities were enacted on Native Americans as well—not only were they confined to their reservations, but in many cases were forced to undergo sterilization or to terminate a pregnancy against their wishes.

This catalogue of institutionalized abuse has left a massive residue of problems among large numbers of Native Americans, the same kinds of problems that were experienced by other indigenous peoples around the world after their lands were settled by Europeans. At the heart of it all is poverty, which often led, and still does lead, to severe health problems. Sometimes these problems are related to alcoholism, ranging from liver disorders to domestic violence. Dietary insufficiency has made obesity commonplace and has led to very high rates of heart disease and diabetes.

Fortunately, the way that the North American governments have dealt with the Native American peoples has, in recent times, changed for the better. Today organizations provide everything from legal support to health advice. Some tribes have become extremely wealthy as a result of oil being found on their lands, while others have built massive gambling empires. All in all, things are improving, and if all goes well, the Native Americans will once again prosper in America.

Fort Laramie

From Nature by A. J. Miller 1856-7

ARCTIC AND SUBARCTIC

The most northerly region occupied by Native American Indians covers the Arctic and Sub-Arctic. Together these two zones form a vast area. The Arctic comprises the territories between the northern edge of the American continent and Greenland, and the Sub-Arctic is made up of the northern interior of Canada and the whole of Alaska. This includes the belt of semi-arctic land from the Rocky Mountains across to Hudson Bay.

The Arctic region remained in the grip of the last ice-age until about 4,000 years ago, after which it was uninhabitable by humans. As the last of the major glaciers in this area melted, people slowly started settling there. Three basic groups of native tribes are found in the region: the Inuit, Yupik, and Aleut. The Inuit (often referred to as Eskimo) can be divided into six further groups: the Greenland Inuit (Kalaallit), Labrador Inuit, Central Inuit, Banks Island Inuit, Western Arctic Inuit (Inuvialuit), and Alaskan Inuit. There are two groups of Yuits—the Alaskan and the Siberian Yuit—and only one group of Aleut.

The native tribes that chose to settle in the very north had to be extremely adept at coping with such a cold climate. Like all human cultures, their two most basic needs were for survival: food and shelter. In a place with no trees and little other vegetation, their resources were very limited. Farming is impossible in the far north because the Arctic winters are too harsh,

and for six months of the year there is little or no daylight. In the sparse woodlands of the southernmost part of the region a certain amount of gathering could be done. At the right time of year berries could be collected, and when the ground was soft enough edible roots could be uncovered. On the ice, however, the choices were few and far between. With the exception of the occasional bird, the only significant source of food was from the sea. This included seals, walruses, and whales. On land, the Indians hunted wildlife, such as caribou and moose.

Although these animals could provide plenty of food, the problem for the hunter was how to catch and kill their chosen prey. For most native tribes the preferred weapon was the bow and arrow, but those who lived on the ice had no trees to make bows and arrows from. The only source of timber was driftwood, which was completely useless for the task. Bows are complicated structures and can only be made from certain kinds of wood. Another challenge was that the extreme cold made most types of wood far too brittle to be used for bow making.

The natives got around this problem in two main ways. The first was to obtain wood from the nearest mainland sources. In the far north the only species of tree that could cope with the low temperatures was birch, although it is not the ideal material for bows. Although it lacked strength, it was less brittle

when it was cold than other woods were. The second solution was to make bows from antler horn. This material also lacks strength, but can cope with the cold. These solutions illustrate just how clever these people were. They used the low-strength materials of birch and antler to construct the body of the bow and to add power they reinforced the bow with complex backings and cables made from whale or caribou sinew. Although the resulting weapon would compare poorly with a longbow of the European settlers and of course of today, it was capable of functioning at very low temperatures. Such a bow could kill a seal at moderate ranges, and this facility made it possible to live out on the ice-sheets.

For those tribes that lived in areas suitable for trapping, it was a productive means of obtaining food. Many different kinds of small animals, from mice to rabbits, could be caught in this way and all were a useful addition to the diet. When the ice on the rivers and lakes melted in spring, traps could also be used to catch fish. Fish could also be taken with spears and fish arrows, and all year long fishing with lines and hooks was undertaken.

In addition to food, shelter was a major priority. The tribes that lived on land made tents from caribou skins, whereas those that lived on the ice constructed igloos from blocks of compacted snow.

When a hunt was successful, every last piece of the animal was used. The meat was eaten on the spot or dried for later use. The skins were cured and used to make clothes, shoes, tents, and all manner of other essential items. The entrails were also used; in the case of caribou, partly digested moss was considered a delicacy and eaten with relish. Certain parts of the gut were dried and used as binding materials for shoe making, tent construction, attaching arrow heads or fletchings, and so on. Glue was made from boiling bones after the sinews had been carefully removed so they could be made into high-strength cordage for all sorts of important uses.

The problem with hunting and gathering is that animals rarely stay in one place for long, and berries are only available at certain times of year. In order to survive, the tribes had to be able to move in response to the changing seasons. Consequently, this meant that their cultures developed into fully nomadic lifestyles. One of the characteristics of nomadic peoples is that the different tribal groups tend to develop different dialects and over periods of time these dialects gradually become distinct languages. In the Arctic and Sub-Arctic region, the main languages are derived from Algonquian-Wakashan and Nadene roots.

AHYOUWAIGHS
CHIEF OF THE SIX NATIONS.

The Aleuts are natives of West Alaska and the Aleutian Islands, which stretch for about 1,100 miles (1,800 km) southwestward from the Alaskan mainland. The Aleut call themselves Unangan, which translates as "the people." Although they are most closely related to the Eskimo and Siberian peoples, their language and culture are different. Before the Europeans arrived on the scene, the Aleut lived in small villages in houses that were partly underground. They had a class system ruled by nobles, at the bottom of which were slaves. Shamans were an important part of the culture. The Aleut were hunter-gatherers. At sea they used lightweight boats covered with skins to hunt fish, seals, sea lions, and whales. On land they searched for eggs, roots, and berries, and hunted for foxes, otters, and birds. They traded a large proportion of the furs they obtained with Russian dealers, many of whom exploited them ruthlessly. Disease caught from incomers had a particularly drastic effect on their population, and it is estimated that today only a tenth of the numbers of Aleut that once existed remain.

AMISKQUEW.

The Athabascan (also spelled Athapaskan) tribes probably arrived in the region as part of the final great migration wave over the last 1,000 years or so. The three tribes that were still in existence in the sub-Arctic region when the Europeans arrived have since all died out. The tribes who spoke Athabascan languages once lived throughout Alaska, Canada, Oregon, California, Arizona, New Mexico, Texas, and as far south as parts of Mexico. Today there are many tribes who still speak Athabascan languages - these include the Chipewyan, Kutchin, Carrier, Hupa, Navajo, and Apaches. In all this amounts to some 175,000 people in Canada and the United States, the majority of which are members of the Navajo tribe.

A.MIS.QUAM,
A WINNEBAGO BRAVE.

The Chipewyan tribe was once the largest group of Athabascan-speaking people. They call themselves Dene, which translates as "people." The name Chipewyan comes from the Cree word meaning "pointed skins." The tribe originally ranged over much of western Canada, along the fringes of the northern forests and well into the tundra areas between the Great Slave Lake and the Churchill River. They were nomadic hunter-gatherers who lived in extended family groups and traveled after the herds of caribou along their seasonal migration routes. They suffered badly when exposed to European diseases, and smallpox in particular took a heavy toll on their numbers. Today some 10,000 living members of the Chipewyan tribe are distributed across Alberta, Manitoba, Saskatchewan, and the Northwest Territories.

CREE

A NA CAM E CLCK CA
A CHIPPEWAY CHIEF.

The Cree were the largest and most important tribe of Native Americans in Canada. They originally inhabited the lands around Lakes Winnipeg and Manitoba and eastward as far as Hudson Bay. The name Cree comes from an Ojibwa word with an unknown meaning. They refer to themselves as Eythinyuwuk, which simply translates as "men." They lived a hunter-gatherer existence, collecting fruit, berries, and roots, much of which would be pounded to remove moisture and then dried and put in storage for later use. They also went on hunting and fishing forays, with buffalo being especially sought after.

The Cree are closely related to the Ojibwa, and until the tribe was greatly weakened by smallpox in the late 1700s, they were one of the most powerful Native American tribes. They had an alliance with the Assiniboin, some of whom joined with members of one Cree faction and moved south to hunt buffalo; they established the plains Cree tribe. The Cree had long-running wars with the Sioux and Blackfeet tribes, among others. They were, however, generally friendly with both the English and French fur traders, who considered them to be good tempered, honest, and generous.

AP-PA-NOO-SE
SAUKIE CHIEF.

The Metis are not a tribe, but a people. When the English, Scottish, and French fur traders reached the Canadian northwest, it was not long before they started interbreeding with women from the local Native American settlements, mostly of the Cree and Ojibwa tribes. Their mixed-blood offspring eventually became so numerous that they evolved into a new and distinct Aboriginal nation known as the Metis people. This expansion began around the mid-1600s and continued to grow until the end of the 19th century. Because the Metis people had roots in both the native and European cultures, they were able to communicate well with both factions. As a result, many established what became very successful companies, transporting provisions the long distances from the towns and ports to the furthest outposts where they were traded for furs. One of their most popular commodities was buffalo meat. A lot of Metis villages were built around the places where the fur trade was practiced, and many of these have since grown into large towns.

The word Eskimo (sometimes spelled Esquimaux) refers to a number of different native groups of the Arctic region that live between the Chukchi Peninsula in northeastern Siberia, across the Bering Strait and over as far west as Greenland. The groups from Canada and Greenland prefer to be referred to as Inuit, which translates as "the people," although many of the native people of Alaska and Siberia do not use the name. Although many distinct Eskimo dialects are used by the many groups across the region, all have very similar cultures. It is believed that the Eskimo people who first crossed into the Americas from northeast Asia were part of the last major migration wave that occurred over the past 5,000 years. They are racially distinct from the Native American Indians; their closest relatives are the Mongolians. The groups that live in the most northerly areas hunt whales and seals, whereas those from the Pacific coast mostly fish for salmon, and those from mainland Canada generally hunt caribou. The population of the Eskimo peoples was around 50,000 when they experienced their first contact with Europeans. Today, the number is about the same.

"Obleka"

NORTHWEST COAST

The northwestern coastal region runs for more than 2,000 miles along the edge of the Pacific Ocean from Alaska to California. It is about 150 miles deep and also includes the Canadian province of western British Columbia as well as the U.S. states of Washington and Oregon. Offshore islands fall into this cultural area as well, stretching from near Yakutat Bay in the north to Washington Strait in the south. The largest of these islands are Vancouver Island, the Queen Charlotte Islands, and the Alexander Archipelago. Along the northern shores of the region are many sheltered inlets, which act as excellent natural harbors. The region includes two major mountain ranges: the Cascades, which are situated in the United States, and the Coast Range in Canada.

The temperate environment is beneficial for human existence, although rather wet. Annual rainfall totals are very high and encourage the large number of trees that cover most of the area to grow prolifically. The first Native Americans arrived on the northwest coast around 12,000 years ago. They found that the area was rich in land animals, as well as in fish, and was home to lots of seed-bearing plants, nuts, berries, and other wild fruits that they could collect for food.

The sea provided a bountiful harvest; fish included salmon, halibut, cod ,and flounder, and marine mammals included dolphins, whales, otters, seals, and sea lions. Fish were used for more than just food. When their bones were boiled, they also provided powerful glues. Almost all the animals that were hunted yielded meat as well as skins and other useful commodities. The land mammals that were on the menu included deer, elk, bears, and mountain goats.

The fact that the sea provided a rich harvest encouraged the native tribes to become excellent inshore mariners. They traveled great distances using canoes and kayaks, and grew to be quite skilled in their use. The tides along the northwest Pacific coast are among the highest in the world, producing incredibly strong currents, which can easily overwhelm a novice.

The tribes had such a plethora of foods to choose from that they did very little farming, with the exception of growing tobacco. The ease of collecting food meant there was plenty of time left over for cultural activities, and the tribes developed complex societal systems. Smoking was part of many social and ceremonial functions, and tobacco was therefore an important crop.

Many large settlements were established along the coast close to the best fishing grounds. These were generally composed of wooden houses, each containing an extended family. The houses themselves were made of substantial frames constructed from tree trunks, which were then planked with wide cedar boards.

Ceremonies and rituals were an important part of community life, and most involved dressing in costumes. Neighboring villages often participated in significant events, the most important of which was a special feast called a potlatch. At these ceremonies affluent individuals gave away many of their possessions, which helped them establish their ranking within the tribe; the higher their rank, the more they gave away. These gatherings encouraged bonding among people and minimized the risk of friction between local tribes.

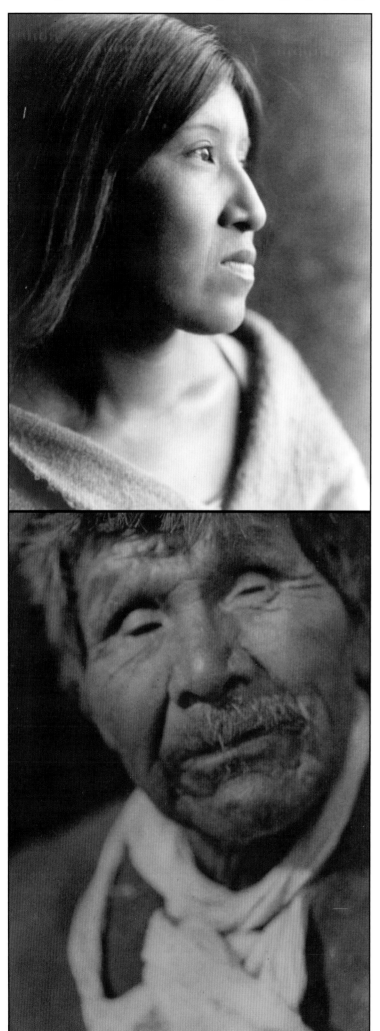

The amount of free time the tribes had on a regular basis is obvious from their artwork. They developed excellent wood-working skills that were put to use in the creation of distinctive wood carvings. Their high carpentry standards were also demonstrated in the construction of cedar-planked canoes and carved dugouts. Today the best-known wooden native artifacts are probably totem poles, carved structures adorned with all sorts of animal decorations and erected in the permanent winter settlements of the tribes in front of each building. The actual animals depicted on the totem poles were carefully chosen by the shamans for their particular significance to the tribe.

The northwestern natives also made many ceremonial art objects, especially masks. Everyday items were also crafted to high standards including baskets made from reeds and woven textiles used to make blankets and clothes. These were often traded among the tribes of the region. Trade—which was popular—was helped by a monetary system based on seashells.

So many different tribes lived in the region that a large number of languages existed alongside one another. In the north, the Na-Dene language family was the most widespread, and the Wakashan and Penutian variants predominated in the central areas.

Although the European settlers first arrived on the East coast at the end of the 1400s, it took them nearly 300 years to make their way across the vast continent of America. Consequently, the Native American cultures that had been in this region for 12,000 years were not significantly disrupted by settlers until comparatively recently, roughly 260 years ago. Sadly, many of the tribes did not survive the exposure to new diseases or to the strange and often hostile ways of the new incomers.

CALIFORNIA

The Native American Indian region known as the California culture area covers most of the United States between the northwest coastal region and Mexico. It includes the southernmost parts of Oregon, most of the state of California, and reaches down to the Baja peninsula into Mexico. The eastern borders are formed by the Sierra Nevada Mountains and the Gulf of California, while the western limits are marked by the Pacific Ocean. A lot of overlap exists between the California culture area and the culture areas of the Great Basin and southwestern areas, as well as the many influences from the northwest and Great Plateau cultures.

The environment in the California culture area varies tremendously depending on the location. The region is characterized by many mountains and a lot of high ground. Two mountain ranges—the Coast Range and the Sierra Nevada—stretch from north southward to Mexico. In the south it is hot and arid, and desert conditions predominate. There are extensive mountain deserts as well, and although these are beautiful places, they provide harsh circumstances in which to try to survive in. Very few rivers flow through the region and often only do so in the winter months.

The more northerly areas enjoy high annual rainfall, and temperatures can drop much lower than in the southern areas. Redwood forests are plentiful and some of the tallest trees in the world can be found in places such as the Yosemite and Sequoia national parks. A byproduct of the high rainfall amounts are many rivers born high in the hills, which gradually wind their way down to the Pacific Ocean. The Native Americans found bountiful natural resources in the region. The rivers and sea offered excellent fishing, and the forests offered the opportunity to hunt all manner of animals, from rabbits to bear, lynx, mountain lion, and deer.

The tribes in the California culture area varied as much as the terrain; most, however, were centered around permanent villages composed of extended families. These villages were presided over by a head man, who organized or advised on everything from ceremonial functions to hunting and fishing expeditions.

ACHOMAWI

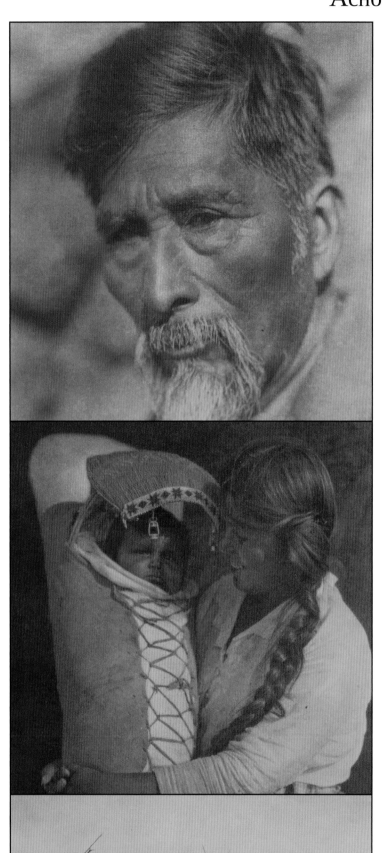

The Achomawi (also spelled Achumawi) were also known as the Pit River Indians, a group of Native Americans that originally inhabited lands in the region of the Pit River in northeast California. The word Achomawi comes from *achoma* in their language, which means river. The river was named Pit by early settlers because of the number of pitfall traps along the trails in the area. The traps were used by the local Indians to catch deer and were very common in the forests of the region, providing an excellent supply of venison as well as skins, sinew, and other products needed by the tribes. Deerskin was used for making many -clothing items including leggings, moccasins, belts, skirts, shirts, caps, and so on. Religion played a key part in the tribe's culture, the central figures of which were shamans, many of whom were women.

NUXALK OR BELLA COOLA

FATHER OLD-SA BLACK HOOF
PRINCIPAL CHIEF OF THE SHAWANOES

The Nuxalk, also known as the Bella Coola, were an ancient group of tribes that inhabited large tracts of land in the region of the central Pacific Coast. They lived among the coastal mountains and fjords for the best part of 10,000 years before the European settlers arrived. Their territories were composed of temperate rainforests and measured close to 9,000 square miles (16,000 sq km). The United States government absorbed these lands. The government's right to the land is still being disputed. In 1995, many tribal members raised a protest in which they blockaded logging operations in an effort to force the authorities to deal with their concerns. These included putting a stop to logging because they believe the forests cannot sustain the demands being made on them to meet the market for timber. They also wanted fishing to be restricted for similar reasons. The protestors were arrested, and their requests were largely unmet. Today about 3,000 members of the Nuxalk survive, about 900 of whom live on the seven reserves they were assigned in the Bella Coola valley area.

CAHUILLA

CHIPPEWAY SQUAW & CHILD

The Cahuilla were a group of Native Americans who inhabited their lands for at least 2,000 years before the European settlers arrived. Their lands covered what is now the Borrego to Riverside areas of California, measuring around 2,400 square miles (3,862 sq km). The tribe was divided into three main groups: the Mountain, Desert, and Pass Cahuillas. Smaller divisions within the groups were identified by particular names, such as the Agua Caliente, Morongo, Los Coyotes, Torres-Martinez, Cabazon, and Santa Rosa Indians.

The men were hunters who used a variety of weapons to capture animals for food. They fashioned bows and arrows and also laid various traps to catch their prey, which ranged from small animals such as rabbit, to bighorn sheep, deer, and antelope. The women were gatherers who collected wild produce such as acorns, cactus fruits, grass seeds, mesquite beans, pine nuts, and so on. Some of the gathered foods were eaten immediately and others were stored away for use during periods of drought or cold weather. Yet others had medicinal or utilitarian uses.

The Cahuilla were similar to many of the other Native American peoples of the region in that they were skilled at making pottery and weaving baskets. Their remote desert location meant that they escaped many of the problems associated with European settlers. Nevertheless, their population was severely diminished by imported diseases. The tribe was believed to be as large as 10,000 in 1862, but after a smallpox epidemic that year only 2,500 or so survived. The Cahuilla are now on 10 reservations in Southern California, and some of the tribe earns income from tourism.

CHEHALIS OR UPPER KWAIAILK

The Chehalis peoples originally occupied large homelands within the Chehalis River Watershed, covering an area from the foothills of the Cascade Mountains across to the Pacific Ocean in southwest Washington state. When it was first used, the name "Chehalis" referred to a group of several different Salishan tribes who lived in the region. Their homes, which were constructed from cedar planks, were situated along the larger rivers and waterways. The rivers and sea provided their main sources of food: salmon, eels, clams, and crayfish. In 1860, the Chehalis were moved onto a reservation that lies across the borders of Thurston and Grays Harbor counties in Washington state. The reservation measures just over 4,200 acres. Although there are now more than 650 living members of the Chehalis Tribe, in 1910 their numbers dropped below 150.

CHITTEE YOHOLO

The Chimakuan were a group of Native Americans from the coastal area of Washington state. By the time European settlers arrived, however, only two tribes of the Chimakuan existed: the Quileute, who still survive, and an eastern tribe called the Chimakum, who are thought to have been wiped out through warfare with other tribes. It is believed that the tribes were once much larger, and that they were driven from their homelands by the Clallani and Makah tribes. Although the Chimakuan were mostly friendly toward white settlers, they had a reputation among other native tribes for their abilities as powerful warriors. They were also very accomplished sailors and derived much of their food by whaling from small boats. The Chimakum still survived into the late 1890s, but they appear to have all since disappeared.

CHON-MON-I-CASE
AN OTTO HALF CHIEF

The Chinook were a tribe of Native Americans whose homelands were situated along the lower Columbian River in Washington state. This waterside location meant that they became expert sailors and fishermen. When the salmon were running in the thousands as part of their spawning cycle, the Chinook were able to catch so many fish that the numbers exceeded what they needed for themselves. As a result, the tribe built a trading network that reached to tribes that lived thousands of miles away. The Chinook also exchanged seashells, which some tribes used as currency, as well as canoes and even slaves. Eventually, they came into conflict with European traders, and their population started to fall. In the end they were forced off their lands and placed on reservations.

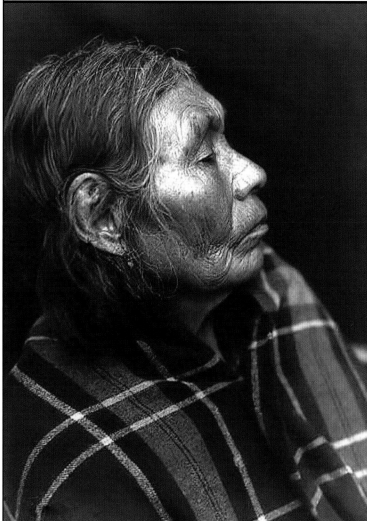

Haida

CHONO CA PE
AN ONIGE CHIEF

The Haida were Native Americans who lived on the Queen Charlotte Islands off the coast of British Columbia, Canada, and on the southern end of the Prince of Wales Island, off the coast of the state of Alaska. Their settlements were composed of large houses that were built from wide cedar planks. They were hunters, catching salmon from the rivers, and hunting for seals, walruses, and other sea mammals from their sturdy dugout canoes. Their tribes were split into two groups: the Eagle and Raven clans. In the days before the white settlers arrived, the Haida numbered around 8,000, but after a series of disease epidemics, particularly smallpox, struck them, their population was reduced to around 2,000 by the late 1870s. Many of the surviving members of the tribe are employed today in the fishing and canning industries.

HOOPA

DAVID VANN.

The Hoopa (also spelled Hupa) tribe formerly occupied lands in the region of the Trinity River between the Hoopa valley and Klamath River in northwest California. They were hunters and gatherers, and were the most southerly based of the Native Americans of the northwest culture area. They traveled extensively along the waterways of the region in dugout canoes looking for places to fish for salmon or to collect wild produce. One of their mainstays was acorns, which they made into a kind of bread. Their settlements contained houses made from wide cedar planks, which had no windows and only a small circular opening as a door. The United States government assigned their lands as a reservation in 1864, where they are still located.

Karok

The Karok (also spelled Karuk) originally inhabited lands on the middle course of the Klamath River, between the Trinity River and the mouth of Bluff Creek, in California, where they had around 36 settlements. They were one of the first peoples to populate the area, some 10,000 years ago. Their name translates as "upstream." The tribe had a nonmigratory hunter-gatherer culture based around salmon fishing, but because redwood trees did not grow in their territories they could not make their own dugout canoes. To solve this problem, they traded with other native tribes for canoes. The Karok suffered badly when gold was discovered on their homelands when the rush of ruthless miners into the region brought conflict and tragedy on both sides. In 1875, the gold seekers killed 75 Karok people, which caused them to move away until the fever for treasure died down. Today the tribe numbers around 2,000 members.

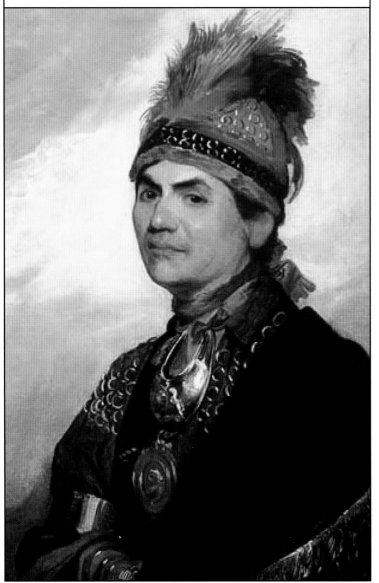

ESH-TAH-HUM-LEAH
or the Sleepy Eye

The Kato or Cahto were the southernmost Athapaskans on the Pacific Coast, formerly inhabiting lands on the upper drainage of the south fork of the Eel River in California where they had 15 to 20 settlements. They were a nonmigratory hunter-gatherer tribe who, like the Karok and other tribes in the area, suffered badly from the influx of gold prospectors in 1850. They also had violent conflicts with the Yuki tribe. These problems conspired to reduce their population from about 500 in 1850 to less than 60 in 1910. Today their numbers have risen to 600 or so, most of whom now live on the Laytonville Reservation.

Kwakiutl (Kwakwala)

The Kwakiutl were a Native American people who inhabited north Vancouver Island and most of the coastline of British Columbia, Canada. They were very skilled woodworkers and became well known for their excellent carvings. These decorative techniques were used to decorate totem poles, gable ends of houses, mortuary posts, masks, and for many other purposes. The Kwakiutl's culture was typical of the Pacific northwest area and included most of the rituals common in the region. The best known of these was the Potlatch ceremony, where valued items were distributed among the tribe.

Kwakiutl (Kwakwala)

TORE-LUITE-HAJO

The Maidu were a widespread group that formerly occupied lands ranging from Nevada to the foothills of the Sacramento Valley. In total, the tribe occupied about 74 settlements. The most southern group—the Nishinam—was in the Bear River Valley and the most northern group was located south of Mount Lassen. Because the area the tribe inhabited was so rich in wild foodstuffs, they did not need to farm, establishing a hunter-gatherer culture. Acorns were a staple of their diet. Acorns were collected and stored in large quantities for later use. Game animals were also plentiful in the woods and forests, and the rivers were full of fish. The Maidu settlements were usually situated such that the trails leading to them could be watched for approaching strangers. The permanent houses that were used in cold weather were large semi-subterranean circular structures built with a pole framework having a thick covering of mud, which made them very warm. Each building would house several families. In the warmer months they would live in more temporary structures made of branches and covered with brush.

Miwok

The Miwok, meaning "man," were Native Americans who were said to be the largest peoples in California. They were split into three culture groups. The Valley Miwok occupied the western slope of the Sierra Nevadas from the Sacramento-San Joaquin delta and Cosumnes River south to the Fresno River. The lands of the Coast Miwok stretched from the Golden Gate north to Duncan's Point and east as far as Sonoma Creek. The Lake Miwok inhabited an area in the basin of Clear Lake. They were hunter-gatherers who thrived until the arrival of white settlers when diseases considerably reduced their numbers. The tribe was almost wiped out entirely when the ravages of disease were compounded by violent conflicts with Mexican and American gold rush settlers.

NOOTKA

The Nootka are a small group of Native Americans who live on the western shore of Vancouver Island, British Columbia, Canada. In the 19th century they were typical of the northwest coast culture, being proficient fishermen who hunted seals, whales, and sea otters in addition to fish. The principle fish species they caught were halibut, cod, and salmon. Gathering wild produce, they collected various berries, roots, and nuts. Although their carving and painting skills were not as developed as those of other tribes in the region, they were expert basket weavers. Before white settlers arrived they numbered around 6,000, but this figure dropped to just over 2,000 at the beginning of the 20th century. Their population has since recovered to more or less the pre-settler level.

POMO

HOO-WAN-NE-KA

The Pomo were a people who lived along the northern California coast in parts of Sonoma, Lake, Mendocino, Colusa, and Glenn counties. The name "Pomo" means "those who live at red earth hole" and may have referred to local deposits of the red mineral magnesite. The Pomo were nonmigratory hunter-gatherers who were generally peaceful both to other tribes and to white settlers. Their basketry skills were possibly the best of all the tribes in North America, and they particularly liked using decorative objects such as feathers to adorn their personal belongings. They suffered at the hands of Russian traders and white missionaries, as well as gold rush settlers. Not only did their numbers dwindle by exposure to disease for which they lacked immunity, but they were moved off of their lands. Their population currently numbers around 800, and many of them live on the Round Valley Reservation.

The Coastal Salish occupied lands along the Pacific coast of British Columbia, from the Strait of Georgia through Puget Sound in Washington state and as far south as the Siletz River in Oregon. The Bella Coola were situated further north along the Burke Channel in British Columbia. The area around the mouth of the Columbia River was, however, inhabited by the Chinook, who were not part of the group. Most of the coastal Salish dwellings were made of wide planks with heavy beams and contained several families, each with its own fireplace. Catching fish from canoes or with nets from the shore, where they also collected shellfish, were mainstay occupations for most of these people. The tribes in this region were not exposed to significant numbers of settlers until much later than most other tribes across America. This was because the ownership of the area was being argued over by the United States and Great Britain. In 1909 there were approximately 8,500 Salish living along the coasts of the United States and Canada.

JOHN RIDGE
A CHEROKEE.

It is believed that the tribes that made up the coastal Shoshone group migrated to the Pacific coast from the Great Basin culture area comprising roughly 400,000 square miles between the Sierra Nevada Mountains and the Rocky Mountains. They occupied lands along the coast in parts of southern California where they had a culture that featured strong religious beliefs based around mysticism. The tribes that composed this group included the Serrano, Gabrieleño, Agua Caliente, Juaneño, Kawia, and Luiseño. All of the tribes had similar methods of obtaining food and their diet consisted of a wide variety of wild produce—such as seeds, acorns, pine nuts, berries, and fruit—and creatures they hunted such as fish, sea lions, deer, and small game animals.

SILETZ

For thousands of years, the Siletz tribe and its ancestors occupied lands in the coastal region of northwestern Oregon in what are now Tillamook, Lincoln, and Lane counties. The Siletz were the southernmost of the Salish tribes of the Pacific Coast, but were forced to move onto a reservation in 1855. The Siletz name was later used to refer to a confederation formed from 27 different tribal bands. These tribes came from a region that stretched from northern California to southwest Washington state and were all moved to the Siletz Reservation in Oregon in 1851. When gold was discovered in the area many thousands of white miners descended in the hope that they would make themselves a fortune. Many of them were very aggressive toward the Native Americans. The reservation was split in two when the government came under pressure to build a railroad through the area. Further reservation lands were lost to settlers, and the authorities managed to take most of the rest by removing their official tribal recognition. After much protest, this was finally reinstated in 1977 with the Siletz Restoration Act.

TLINGIT

The Tlingit (also spelled Tlinget, Tlinkit, and Tlinket) formerly occupied homelands along the coast of southern Alaska and on the many islands off the coast. Fourteen different bands composed the tribe. They were very proficient fishermen and very successful traders. They often traveled into the inland areas of Alaska to get produce from other Native American peoples and transport it back to the coast where it was exchanged with the white traders, who usually only operated in places accessible by boat. In the late 1700s the Russians built a fort on their land, to which the Tlingit objected. Eventually they managed to force the Russians to leave, but when the Russians returned a violent battle ensued and many tribal members were killed. This trouble continued for many years. Today the Tlingit live on reservations in British Columbia and Alaska.

TOLOWA

JULEE-MATELA.
A SEMINOLE CHIEF.

The Tolowa's ancestors arrived in the Pacific northwest from Canada sometime after 1000 AD. The tribe obtained most of its food by fishing. When the white settlers and miners came to the area they brought many virulent diseases with them. The 1850s in particular were a decade of epidemics of measles and cholera. These illnesses reduced the tribe's numbers considerably, and today only about 200 survivors remain; most located on the Elk Valley and Smith River Rancherias in northern California.

The Tsimshian (also spelled Chimmesyan) occupied lands along the coast of British Columbia and north into Alaska. Their culture was typical of the northwest coastal area. They used canoes to fish for cod and halibut at sea, where they also hunted for seals and sea lions. They also caught large numbers of salmon as they moved upstream to spawn each spring and hunted for bears, mountain goats, and deer. Today the Tsimshian remain in their native habitat where they still do a lot of fishing, but also generate some of their income from forestry. About 12,000 tribal members live in Canada and the United States.

KALNAHUMA
AN OTTAWA CHIEF.

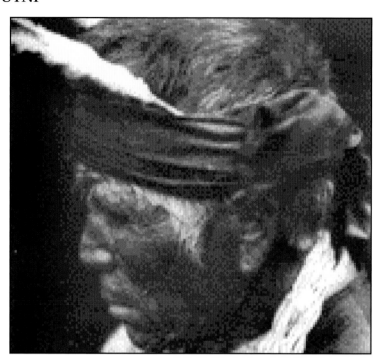

The Tututni originally occupied lands along the Illinois and lower Rogue rivers in southwestern Oregon. They were often referred to as the "Coast Rogues." Their first contact with European explorers was in the early 1790s, and soon thereafter with European traders. These new interactions resulted in many diseases, which reduced their population to around 1,300 by the early 1850s. At this time there were eight groups living on the coast and three along the banks of the Rogue river. In 1857 they were forcibly removed to the Siletz Reservation as prisoners of war.

WAILAKI

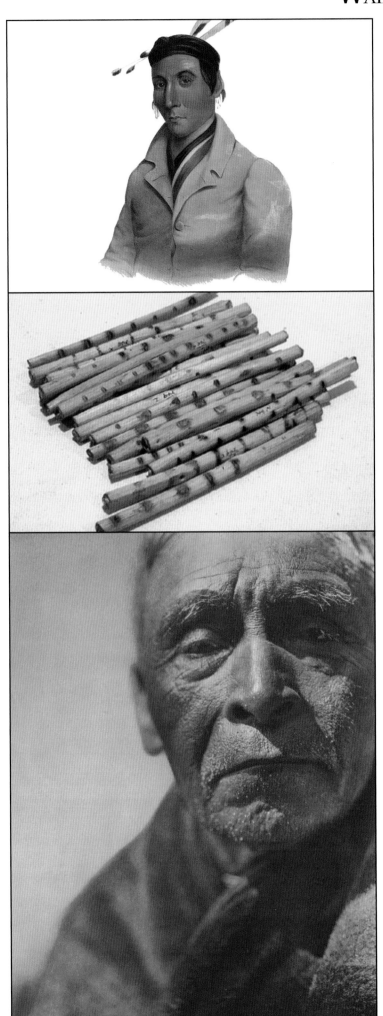

The Wailaki were a Native American people that originally lived on the Eel River as far as the border of Yuki territory at the Big Bend and also lived along several tributaries of the river. Their culture was typical of coastal hunter-gatherers so that fishing provided the mainstay of their food supply. They did not use canoes to fish, but instead used spears and nets. The women collected many kinds of wild produce including roots, seeds, nuts, fruit, and berries, and the men hunted deer and other game animals. Their ancestors arrived on the Pacific coast from Canada soon after the turn of the first millennium. They soon came into conflict with white settlers and were forced to move to the Round Valley Reservation where some of the tribe still live.

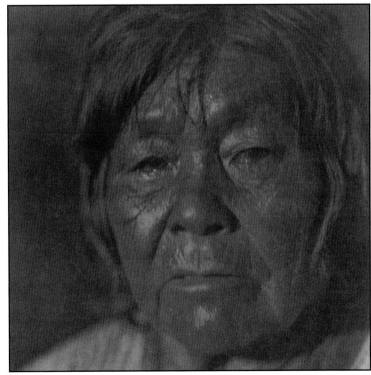

KEE.SHES.WA.

The Washoe (also spelled Washo) originally occupied lands in the region around the Washoe and Tahoe lakes in western Nevada and eastern California. Before this they lived further east, but conflicts with the Northern Paiute forced them to move westward. They were a semi-nonmigratory hunter-gatherer culture that managed to avoid contact with white incomers for a long time. This successful avoidance saved them from the diseases that decimated so many other native tribes. They did, however, lose most of their lands to white settlement. Today the surviving Washoe members live on reservations in California and Nevada.

WILLAPA

KEE-SHE-WAA.

The Willapa were one of a small group of tribes in the Chinookian group of Native American peoples, and their homelands had the most northern location of these peoples. They were situated along the Willapa River and around the Willapa Bay area in Washington state. The Chinookian tribes were skilled fishermen who took advantage of the natural abundance of salmon during the spawning run every spring. They were also active gatherers who dug for roots and collected acorns, berries, and fruit. The men hunted for deer, elk, and game birds. The Willapa tribe are now extinct, although quite when this occurred is not clear.

The Wintun, also known as the Wintu, occupied homelands on the west side of the Sacramento Valley bordered in the north by Mount Shasta. They were hunter-gatherers and very proficient fishermen. Their large catches of salmon were largely dried and stored. They also collected lots of wild produce, including many kinds of roots, berries, pine nuts, and acorns. The tribe suffered terribly from the attempted genocide imposed on them when the area was under Mexican rule and their numbers were further reduced by virulent diseases caught from the gold rush settlers and miners. In recent years their numbers have recovered to a certain extent, and today the tribal population is around 3,200.

WIYOT

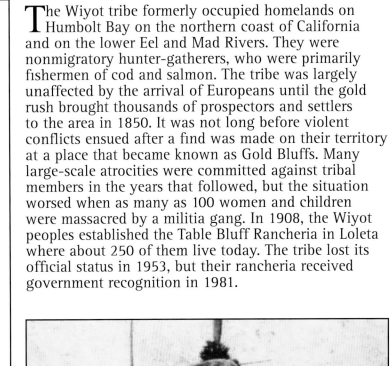

The Wiyot tribe formerly occupied homelands on Humbolt Bay on the northern coast of California and on the lower Eel and Mad Rivers. They were nonmigratory hunter-gatherers, who were primarily fishermen of cod and salmon. The tribe was largely unaffected by the arrival of Europeans until the gold rush brought thousands of prospectors and settlers to the area in 1850. It was not long before violent conflicts ensued after a find was made on their territory at a place that became known as Gold Bluffs. Many large-scale atrocities were committed against tribal members in the years that followed, but the situation worsed when as many as 100 women and children were massacred by a militia gang. In 1908, the Wiyot peoples established the Table Bluff Rancheria in Loleta where about 250 of them live today. The tribe lost its official status in 1953, but their rancheria received government recognition in 1981.

The Yokuts peoples were originally located along the whole length of the San Joaquin valley in central California from the San Joaquin River to the foothills of the Tehachapi mountains and along the edge of the Sierra Nevadas. They were part of a language group known as the Mariposan family; *mariposa* is the Spanish word for butterfly. The group was composed of up to 50 different tribes, and most of them experienced terrible depredations when the area was under Mexican rule, only compounded by mistreatment by the white settlers and miners who followed the Mexicans. Their settlements often had a long communal house with separate entrances for each family. The women were skilled basket weavers, and the men used the bow and arrow to hunt wild game. It is thought that around 2,500 members of the Yokuts peoples are alive today.

YUKI FAMILY

KISH-KE-KOSH

The Yuki originally occupied lands above the north fork of the Eel River in California and some archaeological evidence suggests they were the first native peoples to inhabit the region we now know as California. They were nonmigratory hunter-gatherers who were divided into several tribes. They had a reputation for being warlike, indeed their name means "enemy" in the Wintun language. The Yuki often had violent conflicts with neighboring tribes. When white settlers arrived in the region, the Yuki's aggressiveness led to them being almost completely exterminated. Most of the survivors were moved to the Round River Reservation in 1864. Only about 100 Yuki are alive today.

YUROK

The Yurok originally inhabited lands in the valley of the lower Klamath River and the neighboring coastal areas. The earliest known Yurok archaeological remains have been dated to around 1300 AD. They were nonmigratory coastal hunter-gatherers who obtained most of their food by collecting acorns and by fishing for salmon. They used tusk shells as currency, and as a tribe they thrived until the arrival of white settlers and miners with whom they had many conflicts. Their numbers were reduced by disease epidemics brought to the area by the newcomers, and in 1855 the authorities assigned them a reservation at which time their population numbered around 2,500. This fell to less than 500 in the 1930s, but has since risen to around 2,300. Most of the surviving Yurok members live on the Elk Valley and Trinidad Rancherias and the Yurok Reservation in California.

GREAT BASIN

As the ancestral Native American tribes moved south, many settled in a geophysical area known as the Great Basin. This region covers most of Utah and Nevada, as well as large parts of Colorado, Wyoming, Idaho, Oregon, and California. Small parts of Arizona, New Mexico, and Montana also fall into this zone. As the Great Basin flattens out, it forms what is known as the Plateau region. This covers much of the Rocky Mountains in the northwestern United States and runs into the southern parts of British Columbia. Because the two regions run into each other, they are often considered together.

The Great Basin is a harsh area to survive in. The lower altitudes are mostly composed of desert vegetation such as sagebrush and tough grasses. The higher areas, which border much of the basin, are largely mountain ranges covered with dry pine forests. This arid climate is a product of low rainfall because the area is bound on the eastern side by the Rocky Mountains and on the western side by the Sierra Nevadas. Together these mountain ranges form a barrier to most rain clouds. Temperatures reach both extremes, getting very high in the summer and very low in the winter.

In order to survive in the dry environment of the Great Basin with its sparse vegetation and few animals, the Native Americans adapted to their surroundings. Most lived as typical hunter-gatherers. Although there was some game to be sought, fishing provided a large part of their protein intake. At the right times of year, the local tribes peoples were able to collect large quantities of pine nuts, as well as acorns, grass seeds, wild beans, and many different kinds of berries. Where there was enough water to do so, some tribes also grew basic crops such as squash, corn, and beans.

The lack of consistent resources meant that the tribes were unable to assemble in large numbers except in times of plenty. As a result, most of the tribes lived semi-nomadic lifestyles, spending much of the year split into small family groups. These traveled widely looking for opportunities to gather food. When the times were right, however, large groups would get together for mass hunting sessions. Sometimes these would be to catch and feast on large grasshoppers that swarmed across the land. At other times they would organize drives to chase down larger animals such as rabbits or antelope.

Buffalo were the most sought after prey, but they were too large and too fast to be caught in the open. A single animal was able to provide food for a family group for a long time, so when a herd was in the area, special drives would be arranged. The most effective way of killing buffalo (before the introduction of the horse) was simply to panic them into running over cliffs. Their carcasses were then butchered and removed. After access to horses, however, the method of hunting changed and Native Americans chased buffalo on the hoof, getting close enough to make a kill using the bow and arrow.

The ability to travel long distances using horses meant that Great Basin tribes often ventured out onto the Plains in search of buffalo. If they were due to go hunting, it was customary to ask the spirits for good fortune - this was done by medicine men, who were also known as Shamans. These individuals were very powerful characters within the tribal system - not only did they perform special ceremonies, but they were also relied on to cure the sick and injured.

When a hunt was successful, not only were thanks made to the spirits, but good use was made of every last scrap of the animal. Meat was eaten or dried for later use. Fat was kept for waterproofing skins and for cooking. Wool was collected and used as insulation and for making simple textiles. Skins were made into clothes or used in the construction of shelters called *wickiups*, winter dwellings that are more substantial than those used in the summer.

A wickiup is a small tepee-shaped structure made from a framework of wooden poles covered with a variety of materials ranging from turf sods cut from the ground, to bark or brushwood, or even animal hides. In the warmer months, the wickiups were dispensed with and simple wind-breaks were made from brushwood. The simplicity of these structures meant they were quickly constructed, which allowed the tribes the freedom to move around easily, and they could focus on collecting food rather than building new labor-intensive homes every time they moved.

The clothes worn varied with the temperature. In warmer regions, men wore simple animal-skin breechcloths, and the women wore skirts. In the more northern regions, both men and women wore leggings. The women wore long dresses over the leggings and the men wore thick shirts.

Whereas the introduction of horses was a great benefit to the native peoples of the Great Basin, the appearance of the miners and settlers who brought the horses was not. The newcomers brought livestock that

ate many of the plants the tribes people relied on for much of their food, but even more devastating to their survival was the loss of forests cut down to provide timber and firewood. Without the forests, they lost their source of pine nuts and one of the mainstays of their existence. Things became even more difficult for the Native Americans when gold and silver were discovered in the region. The discovery brought hordes of new settlers to the area and put even more pressure on the natural resources.

One of the biggest problems that the influx of Europeans brought was disease. Just about every illness from smallpox and scarlet fever to influenza worked its way through the native tribes people and countless lives were lost. Today the Native Americans of the Great Basin have largely sorted out their legal rights and have gained full title to large areas of land. Many make their living as ranchers or by leasing out mineral rights to industry.

PLATEAU

The Plateau region is extensive. It covers southeastern British Columbia, the eastern part of Washington, the northeastern and central parts of Oregon, as well as some of northern Idaho, western Montana, and a small part of northern California. Like the Great Basin, which forms the region's southern boundary, the Plateau is bounded on the west and east by two mountain ranges: the Cascades and the Rockies. But unlike the Great Basin, which is largely desert, many parts of the Plateau region are quite humid because the mountains on either side trap most of the rain clouds that form there. The result is a high rate of precipitation. The rainwater collects and runs into the many streams and rivers. The two biggest waterways are the Columbia and Fraser Rivers, but many smaller ones wind through the area. These include the Snake, Okanagon, Willamette, and Kootenai rivers.

The wet climate presents ideal conditions for trees to grow, and many reach enormous heights. In fact, some of the tallest trees in the world are found here. The trees are mostly coniferous species and include cedar,

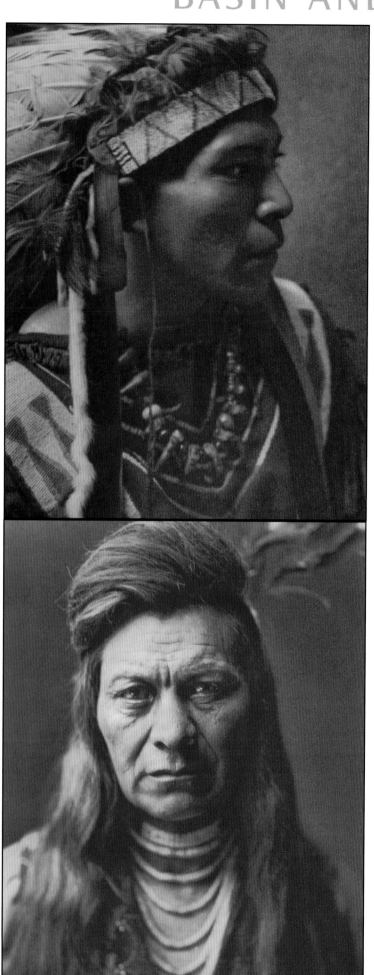

spruce, hemlock, pine, and many others. Like most evergreen forests, the trees grow very close together and very little light reaches the ground. As a result, under the cover of the canopy some areas are very dark places and support very little wildlife. Consequently, in the most wooded areas very few animals live for humans to hunt. Around the fringes, however, large mammals such as deer and elk flourish.

The extensive forests of the upper Fraser River mark the northern limits of the Plateau. Not all the Plateau receives high amounts of rainfall, however, and in the drier areas sagebrush predominates. These regions are largely rolling hills and the vegetation is able to support a good number of antelope and jackrabbits, as well as many other small animal species.

Although the tribes people of the region hunted small game wherever it could be found, a large part of their diet consisted of fish, especially salmon, which were caught in the rich rivers that ran through the region. Some of them were consumed immediately, but most were dried and stored to be traded or eaten later. A large amount of gathering was also undertaken, with berries, nuts, roots, and bulbs collected when they were in season. These were dried and stored whenever possible. Some tribes also made a special kind of bread by grinding acorns.

The people of the Plateau region often lived in brush shelters or lean-to structures that were very similar to those of the Great Basin tribes. They also had more permanent homes, which were half-buried lodges with conical roofs or sometimes wooden long houses covered with tree bark.

When the horse arrived in the early 18th century, the Plateau tribes continued to hunt fish, but they were also able to chase down and kill buffalo. Not only did this give them the ability to feed their families more reliably, but it meant that they could travel further to trade goods. This resulted in significant cultural changes as interactions with other tribes became more commonplace. The choice of materials for clothing became wider, and many went from wearing primitive fabrics made from rabbit skins or woven tree bark, to using much better materials such as deerskin.

Although the Native Americans of the Plateau region generally got on well with white fur trappers and traders, relations went downhill when settlers and miners started taking their lands. They also suffered, like most of the other American tribes, when they were exposed to the virulent diseases brought over from Europe. Eventually wars broke out, as settlers and tribes peoples fought over native lands. The most famous were the Modoc War of 1872–1873 and the Nez Perce War of 1877. Most of the tribes of the Plateau region now live on reservations in Canada and the United States.

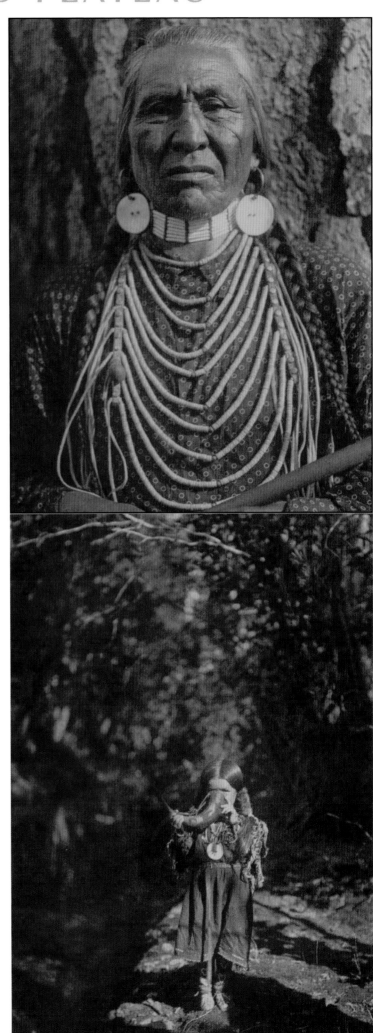

BANNOCK

LAP PA NIN SON.
A DELAWARE CHIEF.

The Bannock were a Native American tribe who lived in large territories that covered parts of the northern Great Plains and the foothills of the Rocky Mountains. They were primarily based in the southern regions of what today is the state of Idaho, where their lifestyles and cultures were similar to those of most of the other Plains Indians. A reservation, named the Fort Hall Reservation, was created for the Native Americans of Idaho in 1869. The Bannock tribe shared these government-appointed lands with the Northern Shoshone, a tribe they had close links with. A Bannock tribe uprising in 1878 erupted in protest at the loss of hunting grounds, but it was quickly controled. A small number of the Bannock people have survived to this day, although they number less than 5,000.

CAYUSE

The Cayuse tribe originally inhabited parts of upper Oregon and southeastern Washington along the Columbia River. They were a very proud tribe, and although they called themselves "the Superior People," the neighboring tribes referred to them as "People of the Rocks." The Cayuse had many enemies due to their habit of preying on smaller tribes in the region, but not all tribes were their enemies; they had particularly good relations with the Nez Perce tribe. The Cayuse brought about their own demise as a free people when in 1847 they attacked a Christian mission and killed the missionaries after blaming them for an outbreak of disease. The local settlers were outraged and declared war on the tribe. After their defeat, the tribe was moved to the Umatilla Reservation in Oregon. Today only a few true Cayuse still survive, and most live on the reservation as part of the Umatilla Federation.

The Flathead tribe, also known as the Salish, formerly occupied northern areas of Washington and Idaho, western Montana, part of the coast of Oregon, the southeast part of Vancouver Island, and most of southern mainland British Columbia. There were two distinct groups of Flathead peoples: one on the northwest Pacific coast, and the other from the interior plateau region. Their name derives from the fact that some of the other tribes of the Columbia River region practiced head shaping—infants had their heads bound with straps to alter the shape of the skull. As a result, the members of these other tribes had pointed heads. The unmodified skulls of the Flatheads marked them as being culturally backward, and the name was therefore a term of derision. For most of their early history, the Flatheads were gatherers who collected berries and roots, but once they made peace with the Blackfeet tribe, whose territory stood between them and buffalo country, they adopted more of a Plains culture. In 1909 there were just over 10,000 plateau Flathead people living in the United States and Canada.

KLIKITAT

The Klikitat tribe was formed by ancestors who came from the Shahaptian-speaking peoples. They originally came from the Klickitat and Skamania counties in Washington state. Their name was given to them by the Chinook Indians and means "beyond," referring to the fact that the Klikitat lived on the other side of the Cascade Mountains from the Chinook. In the early 1800s, the Klickitat tribe was estimated to have about 700 members. They were very successful traders, an attribute that was helped by the fact that their tribal lands were between the Cascade Mountains and the coast. This allowed them to profitably transport all manner of goods back and forth. The remaining members of the tribe are now mostly living on the Yakima Reservation in Washington state.

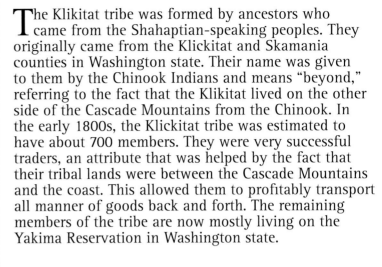

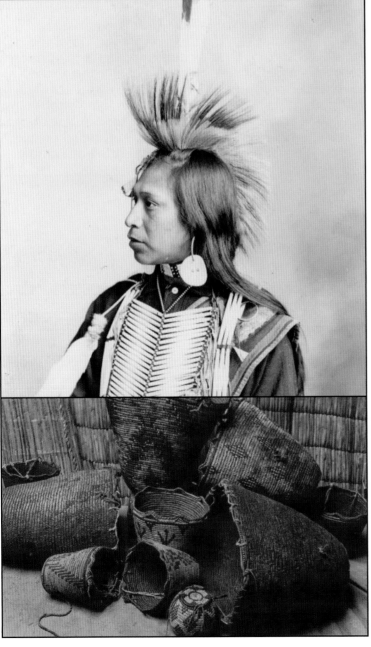

KUTENAI

LE SOLDAT DU CHENE.
AN OSAGE CHIEF.

The Kutenai (also spelled Kootenai or Kootenay) formerly inhabited areas of northern Montana, northern Idaho, and southeast British Columbia. This region was known as the Kutenai and hence is the derivation of the tribe's name. The tribe were split into two main groups: the Upper Kutenai occupied lands around the headwaters of the Columbia River, and the Lower Kutenai inhabited the region of the Lower Kutenai River. Before the introduction of the horse, the Kutenai lived as hunter-gatherers, but once they were able to chase buffalo from horseback they adopted a Plains lifestyle. Their first consistent contact with Europeans was with traders from the North West Company, who established a trading post on the upper Saskatchewan River. A small group of Kutenai people live on the Flathead Reservation in northwest Montana.

MONO

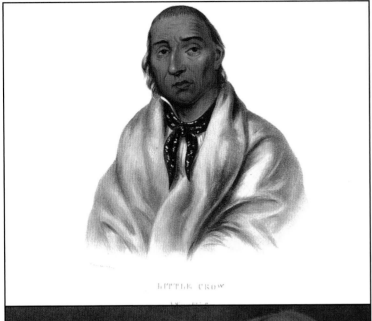

LITTLE CROW

The two main branches of the Mono are the eastern, or Owens Valley, Paiute who lived in the southern Sierra Nevadas and the western Mono or Monache. These two branches comprise a group of six small Shoshonean-speaking tribes that are now part of the mixed Tula River Reservation group.

MA HAN KAH
CHIEF OF THE IOWAYS

The Nez Perce are also referred to as the Sahaptin or Shahaptin peoples. In the early 1800s, they occupied lands in west Idaho, northeastern Oregon, and southeastern Washington. The name Nez Perce comes from the French; it means "pierced nose" and refers to the fact that some members of the tribe wore nose pendants. Their early culture was very much that of the hunter-gatherer. They fished for salmon, dug for roots, and hunted for small animals. Once they acquired the horse, however, they took on many of the Plains Indian practices such as hunting buffalo. They also became accomplished horse breeders and traders. They fared badly when the gold rush of the 1860s and 1870s brought thousands of miners and settlers onto their lands, and many territorial disputes resulted.

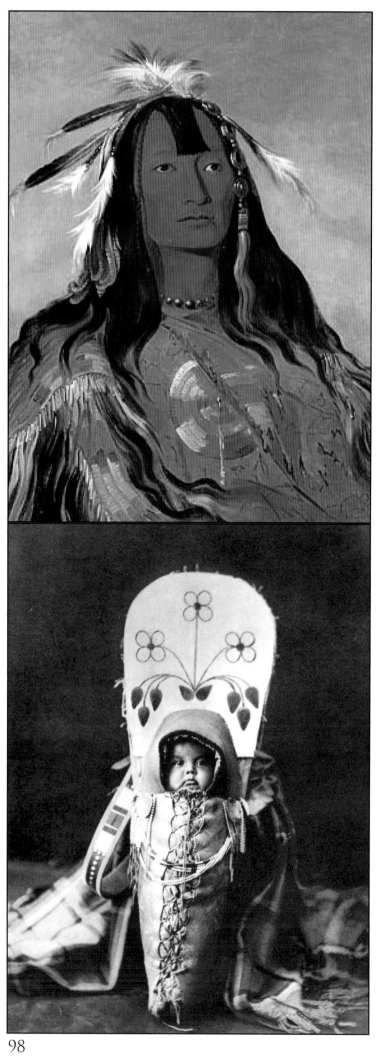

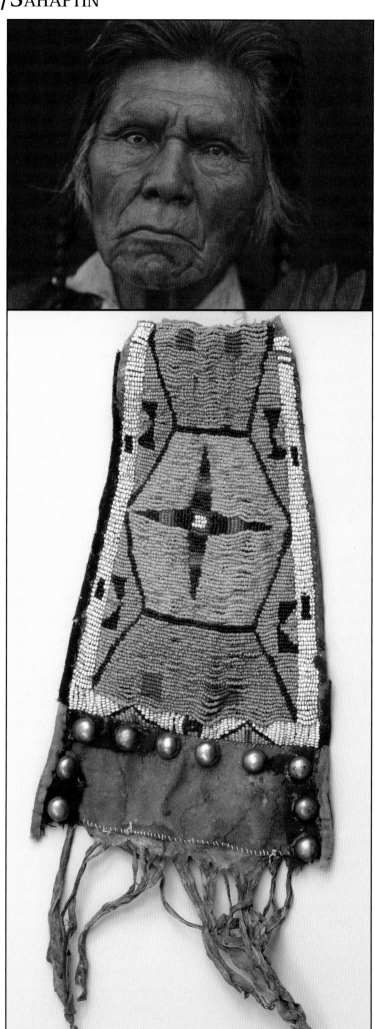

PAIUTE

MAJOR RIDGE.

The Paiute (also spelled Piute) tribe lived as two separate groups. The Northern Paiute inhabited the lands of central and eastern California, western Nevada, and eastern Oregon. The southern Paiute lived in northwestern Arizona, southeastern California, southern Nevada, and southern Utah. Of the two groups, the northern people were the more aggressive. They had many fights with settlers and miners during the mid-1800s. The southern Paiute had a completely different culture. They were hunter-gatherers who got much of their food by digging for roots and were known as "the diggers." They would, however, also fish and hunt small animals when the opportunity presented itself. Today the remaining Paiute live on reservations in Arizona, California, Nevada, and Oregon.

MAR-KO-ME-TE.
A SHOSHONE BRAVE.

The Shoshone family is a group of associated native peoples that occupied the third-largest tribal area in North America. At one time or another this region included southwestern Montana, most of southern Idaho, all of Utah and Nevada, southeastern Oregon, central and western Wyoming, central and western Colorado, much of New Mexico, and all of northwestern Texas. Other Shoshonean lands included disjointed parts of California and northern Arizona. This massive area covers almost all the different kinds of climate and terrain that can be found between Mexico and Canada. Consequently, the various tribes that lived there had to adopt differing lifestyles to suit the kinds of environments they inhabited. Some were primarily hunters of large game animals, whereas others subsisted on roots, berries, and small animals. The Shoshonean family itself was composed of many tribes, which could be divided into three main groups. One is the Plateau Shoshoneans: the Chemehuevi, Kawaiisu, Paiute, Panamint, Ute, Comanche, Gosiute, Mono, Paviotso, part of the Bannock, and the Shoshoneans of eastern Oregon. The second group encompasses the southern Californian Shoshoneans and included the Serrano, Gabrieleño, Agua Caliente, Juaneño, Kawia, and Luiseño. The third group is made up of the Hopi peoples, who are considered to be distinct from the other two groups.

The Spokane peoples occupied several small territories near the Spokane River in northeast Washington state. Opinions differ as to how they should be classified. Most authorities consider them to be distinct bands and not a single tribe. They lived in a manner typical of the plateau people, hunting and gathering as the opportunities arose. At the end of the 19th century they were given two reservations: the Colville Agency in Washington and the Coeur d'Alene Reservation in Idaho. Their population has always been small. Between 1800 and 1910 it varied from around 400 to about 600. This has since risen to around 2,000, with members living on both the reserves in Washington and also in Idaho and Montana.

META-KOOSEGA
Pure Tobacco
A Chippewa Warrior

The Umatilla are a tribe from the Shahaptian linguistic family, although their language differs from the others. They originally inhabited parts of the Columbia River Plateau in northeastern Oregon and southeastern Washington, along the banks of the Columbia River. In 1855, they agreed to a treaty that gave them the Umatilla Reservation in eastern Oregon. They banded together with the Cayuse and Walla Walla tribes to form the Confederated Tribes of the Umatilla Indian Reservation. It is difficult to know exactly how many members of the tribe still survive due to the continued presence of the other tribes who still also live on the same reservation. Estimates put the number of true-blood Umatilla at 250 or less, although the confederation as a whole currently numbers around 2,500 people.

DIE NA WA.
A CREEK WARRIOR.

The Ute tribe originally inhabited Colorado and eastern Utah, however, once they obtained horses they moved further afield and started hunting through Mexico and Arizona. They were fierce warriors who often raided and sometimes destroyed the villages of the Pueblo peoples. They became slave traders, capturing members of other tribes and selling them in slave markets in New Mexico. They were relocated onto a reservation in Colorado in 1868 and moved again in 1880 when it was discovered that the land they were on was rich in minerals. Most of the remaining Ute live on reservations in Colorado and Utah, where they earn money by leasing land for oil and gas extraction as well as by more traditional methods such as farming.

ME . TE . A,
A POTTAWATOMIE CHIEF.

The Walla Walla are another tribe from the Shahaptian linguistic family. They originally lived in Washington and Oregon on the lower Walla Walla River and along the eastern bank of the Columbia River. Their language is a unique dialect that is most closely related to that of the Nez Perce. They agreed to be moved to the Umatilla Indian Reservation in 1855. They remain there today and the current population is around 460. This reserve covers around 160,000 acres. Over the years, however, the Walla Walla have intermarried with members of the Nez Perce, Cayuse, and Umatilla tribes, so it is possible that the true blood line may no longer exist.

MICANOPY
A SEMINOLE CHIEF.

The Yakima used to inhabit lands along the Columbia and Yakima rivers in central Washington state. They lived as typical hunter-gatherers and subsisted on various foodstuffs including salmon and many kinds of roots, berries, fruits, and nuts. When the United States government tried to move them off their lands and onto a reservation in 1855, the Yakima initially agreed to go. When they discovered that the authorities had tricked them, they started a war. The war continued until 1859, when they finally agreed to move to a reservation in southwestern Washington state. They used to refer to themselves as the Toppenish, but in the 1990s the tribe was renamed the Yakama because it fits the pronunciation more accurately. Today the tribe generates most of their income through forestry.

PLAINS AND PRAIRIE

The Great Plains culture area is a vast grassland that stretches from the west of the Mississippi Valley across to the foothills on the eastern side of the Rocky Mountains. It is bounded in the north by the Canadian provinces of Manitoba, Saskatchewan, and Alberta. The southern boundary is formed by the state of Texas. Most of the area is open grassland, but many small stands of willows and cottonwood trees dot the banks of the rivers and streams that criss-cross the region. The mountain ranges in the region include the Ozarks in Missouri, the Badlands in North Dakota, and the Black Hills in South Dakota and Wyoming.

Before the arrival of Europeans—an era known as "pre-Columbian"—the native tribes fell into two main categories: nomadic and nonmigratory. The nomads moved on foot to follow the buffalo herds. They often used bush fires to force the herds into enclosures where they could be easily killed. This was a harsh existence, because of the difficulty in keeping pace with the herds and many drives failed. As a result, the natives went through cycles of hunger and plenty. When a drive was successful, they were able to trade the meat and skins with local farming tribes for grain and other crops.

The tribes that chose to create permanent settlements did so where the ground was suitable for farming corn, various kinds of beans, and squash. Fertile land was found mostly in the valleys of the great rivers. In these locations, the tribes of the plains and prairies built substantial homes to house their extended families. Typically, the structures were dome-shaped lodges with thick walls constructed from compacted mud. For protection from the strong winds and from enemy attack, most of the villages were surrounded by massive earthen walls. Other tribes, such as the Mandan tribe, were semi-nomadic and used tepees when they left their villages to go hunting. A tepee was a tent-like conical structure made of poles and covered with buffalo skin.

On the eastern side of the region where the rainfall is heaviest—between 20 and 40 inches annually—the prairie grasses grow very tall. Toward the western areas, however, where the rainfall is much lower—only about 10 to 20 inches annually—the grasses are much shorter. The prairies are ideal grazing grounds for herbivorous animals, none more so than the buffalo. As the last ice-age receded, these large animals flourished in the enormity of the grasslands. Because their main natural predators became extinct with the climatic changes at the end of the ice-age, the buffalo population increased so dramatically that when the first Europeans arrived a single herd could stretch from horizon to horizon.

As with the native tribes in the other culture areas that had access to buffalo, these animals represented not only a supply of meat but also a source of many other vital commodities. Until the horse was introduced by Spanish explorers, the Plains Indians had to hunt on foot and could only manage to make the occasional kill. Once they were mounted on horseback, however, they were able to chase and kill as many buffalo as they wanted. Any meat that wasn't destined to be eaten

in the short term was cut and pounded into flat strips and then dried. In this state it could be stored for use later or traded for other commodities.

The transition from foot to horseback happened around the early 1700s. It marked a profound change in the lifestyles of almost all the native tribes in the region. Many of the previously nonmigratory peoples found that because horses gave them the ability to keep up with the buffalo herds, it was more productive to hunt than to farm. As a result many tribes gave up farming altogether and took to a nomadic hunter-gatherer lifestyle. Exceptions to this were the Arikara, Hidatsa, and Mandan tribes.

It is important to realize that the Native American perspective on the connection between the spirit world and their own daily existence meant that every animal was seen as sacred. This had important implications for the buffalo herds, because the native hunters would only kill what they needed and no more. Once the Europeans came on the scene, however, they viewed the seemingly endless herds as an infinite resource, and they killed everything in sight. Before long, the numbers of buffalo had been reduced to the point that they were facing extinction.

The history of the tribes of the Great Plains and Prairie culture region is long and complicated. It can be divided into three main periods. The first is the era of hardship before the advent of the horse and stretches from antiquity to the late 1600s. The second is the "time of plenty" after horses were obtained in the early 1700s, but before European settlers made their mark. The third is the post-conquest period from when settlers took control of the region in the mid 1800s until the present day.

The tribes that roamed the plains on horseback following the herds of buffalo were generally composed of groups of related families. During the winter these groups would split up and the families would independently strike out to look for food. In the summer the families would assemble to hunt for buffalo en masse. Once rejoined, religious celebrations would be held. The Native American peoples believed in personal spirit guides. These guides would visit them during vision quests, which were ritual events held to commune with the spiritual world. Some tribes used "medicine bundles," which were sacred pouches carried by certain members of the tribe that contained various objects believed to possess special powers. These objects could be plants, stones, or artifacts that were, for various reasons, judged to have the necessary spiritual significance.

The Sun Dance was a particularly important religious ceremony to the tribes of the Great Plains. It was the time when thanks were made for the good things that happened in the last year, and blessings were asked for the forthcoming year. This and other rituals are still performed to this day by many of the Plains Indian tribes.

PLAINS AND PRAIRIE

Some people refer to the Plains region as one entity, whereas others maintain that the cultures of the semi-nomadic farmers on the prairies and those of the hunters on the plains are so different that the culture area needs to be treated as two separate regions. In this case the dividing line is the course of the lower Mississippi and central Missouri rivers.

Many of the earliest native tribes to settle in the region established farming communities because hunting on foot on the Plains was usually very unproductive. Growing food was therefore considered to be a much more reliable way of feeding their families. Such tribes included the Mandan and Hidatsa, who spoke Siouan languages, and the Wichita, Pawnee, and Arikara, who spoke variants of the Caddoan language family.

With the arrival of the horse, other tribes moved in from the east lured by the enormous herds of buffalo. These included the Arapaho, Cheyenne, Crow, Gros Ventre, Osage, Otoe, Quapaw, and Sioux peoples. Many of these tribes made the move onto the Plains because they were feeling the pressure of the European settlers who were moving onto their traditional homelands. In addition, many severe droughts in the eastern lands made life there difficult. It was not only from the east that new native tribes came in search of buffalo. The Sioux moved in from the Great Lakes area, and the Comanche and Kiowa moved onto the Plains from the west and northwest. The Navajo and the Apache moved up from the southwest.

The diversity and complexity of the languages in the region meant that communication was very difficult. This made trading or simply remaining on good terms with your neighbors a confusing affair. As a result, a simple universal sign language was developed, and this became popular throughout the culture area.

When the European settlers reached the Plains, the only true nomads were the Blackfeet tribes in the northern parts of the region and the Comanche in the southern areas. All the other tribes were either farmers in permanent villages or semi-nomadic tribes who returned to more permanent settlements between excursions.

The Plains Indians were among the last to carry on fighting the settlers. In 1890, the on-going conflict culminated in the battle of Wounded Knee, South Dakota, where the Federal soldiers of the U.S. Army massacred as many as 300 Sioux men, women, and children. After this the Plains Indians became the focus of much media attention, and thus the public came to associate all Native Americans with those from the plains.

These days things have changed, for instance, many Sioux members are now heavily involved in the American Indian Movement, which is an organization that fights for the Native American's legal and civil rights. Others, including many members of the Cheyenne and Comanche tribes are now playing leading roles in the Native American Church.

There are three main language families in the Plains and Prairie culture area: the Algonquian-Wakashan, Aztec-Tanoan, and Hokan-Siouan.

MISSOURI INDIANER.

OTO INDIANER.

CHEF DER PUNCAS.

Indien Missouri.

Indien Oto.

Chef des Puncas.

ARAPAHO

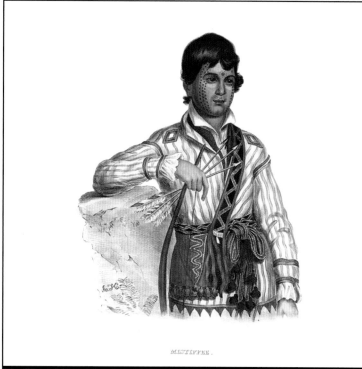

MISTIPPEE.

The Arapaho (also spelled Arapahoe, Arrapaho, or Arrapahoe) are thought to have migrated onto the Plains area from the Red River Valley in North Minnesota. Evidence also suggests that they are closely related to the Blackfoot and Cheyenne peoples, however, little is actually known of their early history. Although they called themselves the "Inuna-ina," which translates as "our people," other tribes labeled them after one of their culinary habits as the "dog eaters." At some stage after their arrival on the plains, they split into three groups: the Gros Ventre, Northern Arapaho, and Southern Arapaho. The Northern Arapaho group, considered to be the parent group from which the others split, remained around the North Platte River in Wyoming. In 1876, they were moved to the Wind River Reservation in Wyoming, where they now live alongside their former enemies, the Shoshone.

The Southern Arapaho, who settled around the Arkansas River in Colorado are now living with the Cheyenne in Oklahoma. The Gros Ventre, which translates from the French as "Big Belly," were split into two further groups: the Atsina and the Hidatsa (also spelled Hinatsa). The Atsina were originally allied with the Blackfoot tribe. Today around 2,800 members survive, most of whom live with the Assiniboin on the Fort Belknap Reservation in Montana. The Hidatsa, who were also known as the Minitari, lived in settlements composed of round houses made from mud, around which was a large earthen wall. They obtained their primary foodstuffs by farming corn and hunting for buffalo. The tribe was badly hit by a smallpox epidemic in 1837, after which it moved up the Missouri River and settled near the Fort Berthold trading post in North Dakota, where many of their descendants still live.

ARIKARA

The Arikara (also spelled Arikari) originally occupied homelands along the course of the upper Missouri River, perhaps settling there as early as the 1300s. The tribe was a semi-migratory group that lived in earthcovered lodges during the spring and summer. During these months they tended their crops of corn, beans, and squash. Surplus foods were traded with other tribes for buffalo meat and hides. When the colder weather arrived, they would de-camp and track the buffalo herds. They were moved to the Fort Berthold Reservation in North Dakota in the late 1800s, where many of them still reside alongside the Mandan and the Hidatsa tribes.

ASSINIBOINE AND STONEY

MOA-NA-HON-GA.
Great Walker.
AN IOWAY CHIEF.

The Assiniboin formerly inhabited the valley regions of the Saskatchewan and Assiniboin rivers in Canada. Later they moved to central North America, in and around the area of northern Minnesota, a land of coniferous forests and numerous lakes. Their name translates from a Chippewa expression as "one who cooks with heated stones." They have also been referred to by several other names; the Hidatsa called them "long arrows," the French called them "rebels," the English "Stone Indians," and the Kutenai "cut-throats."

The Assiniboin were nomads and lived in tepees, lightweight tents made from a skin-covered framework of poles. A tepee was easy to set up and take down in a hurry, a vital attribute because much of the year the tribe had to move constantly to follow the buffalo herds. Some of the tented settlements were quite large, and could be composed of up to 200 tepees with the bigger ones often housing more than one family. During the winter the tented villages moved less frequently because the animals the tribe hunted in the winter did not move large distances in the same way the buffalo did.

In the cold months, their quarry would mostly be antelope, deer, elk, and bighorn sheep. While the men were out hunting, the women would collect berries, roots, nuts, and fruit. Although the Assiniboin were one of the largest tribes in the region, smallpox brought by the white settlers reduced their population to the point they were unable to protest when they were forced onto a reservation in western Montana. Unfortunately, the United States government failed to deliver promised food supplies and many hundreds more starved to death. The remnant of the tribe now lives on reservation lands in Canada and Montana.

The Blackfoot, also known as the Blackfeet, were a group of Plains Indians composed of three main tribes: the Siksika (also spelled Siksikawa), who are considered to be the "true" Blackfoot; the Piegan; and the Kainah. Piegan translates as "people having badly dressed robes" and Kainah means "blood." In the early 1800s these peoples inhabited lands that ranged across a wide area around the upper Missouri and north Saskatchewan rivers and west as far as the Rockies.

The name Blackfoot was applied to them because they dyed their moccasins black. The tribe was nomadic and very hostile to almost all of the other local native peoples, although they did form a close alliance with the unrelated Atsina tribe. They were also usually aggressive toward white settlers. In spite of this, they grew rich by doing business with European traders, usually lucrative deals revolving around the exchange of beaver pelts for firearms and other modern commodities. But the tide turned in the mid-1800s when large numbers of white hunters came into the area armed with powerful guns and reduced the population of buffalo and beaver to such a degree that the Blackfoot people were left with no furs to trade and no meat to eat. This turn of events put them in a very difficult situation, and many of their people suffered as a result. The tribe fell from 3,700 in 1858 to around 2,500 three years later. Today their descendants live on reservations in Montana and Alberta, Canada.

The Cheyenne (also spelled Cheyanne) formerly inhabited lands in the Minnesota region, but problems with the Sioux and Ojibwa tribes in the 1600s forced them to move southwest to avoid further conflict. When they acquired the horse, they became nomadic buffalo hunters.

In the early 1800s they split into two groups: the Northern and the Southern Cheyenne. The Northern group stayed in the territories they had occupied along the upper Platte River since moving away from Minnesota 200 years earlier. The Southern group, however, settled along the Arkansas River, where they allied with the Arapaho and engaged in constant warfare against the Kiowa, Comanche, and Apache. A peace treaty was finally brokered around 1840, whereupon the five tribes became allies. Although they were hostile toward many of the other native tribes, they generally got on well with the white settlers. This changed when the gold rush brought large numbers of gold seekers into their territories.

In the early 1860s the Cheyenne were forced to accept relocation to a reservation in Oklahoma, but the authorities did not provide promised food and the tribe starved. In order to feed their people, they raided many local farms. In 1864, in response to these raids, the U.S. Army massacred a large number of the Cheyenne people, including men, women and children, at Sand Creek, Colorado. The conflict waged on for years and culminated in 1876 at the famous Battle of the Little Bighorn, where the Northern Cheyenne aided by the Sioux massacred General Custer and the 7th Cavalry. After this they were defeated and moved to the same reservation in Oklahoma as the Southern Cheyenne. This was a very difficult time for them, and their numbers fell drastically as a result of disease and malnutrition. Today most of the tribe are settled on a reservation in Montana.

STANDING ELK — N°1
RUNNING HOG — 2
LITTLE WOLF — 3
COL. OELRICHS — 4

CHEYENNE

127

COMANCHE

"Tachkoniy" Comanche

The Comanche was a tribe whose original culture was typical of the Basin Indians. But after they acquired the horse, the Comanche split from the Shoshone tribe and moved southward to New Mexico, where they soon adopted a Plains culture. By the late 1700s their territories covered southeast Colorado, southwest Kansas, western Oklahoma, and northern Texas. They refer to themselves as Numunuh, which means "the people." The name Comanche is derived from Komantcia, the name the Spanish used for them which means "anyone who wants to fight me all the time." Obviously, they were a very warlike people. They often went on long-distance raids as far south as Mexico, and it is said that for a tribe of their numbers they killed more white people than any other Native American group. The combination of their superb skills as horsemen and their aggressive nature prevented white settlers from traveling across their lands for over 100 years. Their population suffered badly from exposure to European diseases and from losses through warfare, so that their numbers fell dramatically.

CROW

The Crow Indians originally inhabited lands around the upper Missouri River until they moved westward in the early 1700s before finally settling in the Wyoming area. Their culture was that of Plains Indians, with their lives being focused on hunting buffalo. They did, however, plant crops of tobacco, which was an important part of their complex religious and social activities. The Crow were long-term enemies of the Sioux tribe and were also aggressive toward the first groups of European settlers who traveled along the Oregon Trail. Although they continued to fight the Sioux, they eventually made peace with the white pioneers and became close allies of the U.S. Army in the Sioux Wars. Many Crow warriors became scouts, and some served with the Seventh Cavalry under General Custer. Today most of the 9,000 or so Crow peoples live on a large reservation to the north of the Montana-Wyoming border, where many earn a good living through ranching and tourism, as well as by leasing out rights for extracting mineral resources.

CROW

GROS VENTRE OR ATSINA

Also known as the Atsina, the Gros Ventre were once considered part of the Arapaho. The Gros Ventre, meaning "big belly," were named by the French. Close allies of the Blackfeet, their history is closely interwoven with their powerful neighbors. Today they share the Fort Belknap Reservation with the Assiniboine.

GROS VENTRE OR ATSINA

139

MON-CHONSIA.
A KANSAS CHIEF.

The Hidatsa, also known as the Minitaree, is a Siouan tribe that was badly affected by smallpox in 1837. Sometimes called the Gros Ventre of the Missouri—and confused with that tribe—they were an earthlodge-dwelling people and thus became the intermediaries between the Plains nomads and the fur trade. They were visited by Lewis and Clarke's expedition and moved to Fort Berthold after the epidemic. They are still there, closely linked with the Mandan.

ASSEOLA.
A SEMINOLE LEADER.

It is thought that the Iowa (also spelled Ioway) were originally part of the Winnebago peoples when they lived in the area north of the Great Lakes. It is known that by 1700 they were living in Minnesota when their population was estimated to be 1,100, but after a particularly bad epidemic of smallpox, they moved again. By the early 1800s their numbers had fallen to about 800, and they were inhabiting lands in the region of the Platte River. The United States authorities took advantage of their weakened state, and in 1824 forced the Iowa tribe to hand over all their territories in Missouri. Instead they were given a reservation in northeast Kansas, although some of the tribe later chose to move to Oklahoma.

Kiowa

NAH-ET-LUC-HOPIE.

The Kiowa were a nomadic people of the Plains who lived in West Montana in the early 1600s, but by the start of the 1700s had settled in a region to the southeast of the Yellowstone River. The Crow tribe gave them permission to live in the Black Hills, but the Cheyenne and Sioux tribes drove them out and they moved south to avoid further conflict. They took up residence in territories that belonged to the Comanche with whom they soon involved in a state of warfare. After much violence between the two peoples, a permanent peace settlement was finally agreed in 1790. In the early 1800s the Kiowa moved to lands in the region of the Arkansas River. In the course of the next three decades they formed an alliance with the Comanche and took part in a lot of long-distance raiding parties. They were very hostile to white settlers, and many conflicts occurred during this time. The U.S. government finally managed to put a stop to most of the aggression in the late 1830s, when a treaty to allow the passage of white pioneers across their lands was agreed upon. Subsequently, the Kiowa, in alliance with several other tribes, started to fight the tribes that had been forced by the government to move to Oklahoma. These battles continued for a long time, but the U.S. Army managed to defeat the alliance and the Treaty of Medicine was imposed on the allied tribes in 1867. By the end of the 1870s most of the Kiowa had moved to a reservation in Oklahoma where many of their descendants still live.

MANDAN

In the mid-1700s, the Mandan lived in the region of the mouth of the Heart River in southcentral North Dakota, where they had a collection of nine settlements. It is believed that they originally came from further east. They were weakened by epidemics of smallpox, and this left them open to attacks by the Assiniboin and the Sioux tribes. To escape further hostilities they moved up the Missouri River and settled near the Arikara tribe around the Knife River. The Mandan numbered around 1,250 in the early 1800s, but by the late 1830s disease had reduced their population to only 150. They were allies of the Hidatsa, and in 1845 both tribes moved to the Fort Berthold trading post in North Dakota. In 1870 a large reservation was created for the Mandan, Arikara, and Hidatsa tribes to share.

OMAHA

The Omaha were a typical Plains Indian tribe who were closely associated with the Ponca peoples. Both groups originally lived in the Ohio Valley, but moved together to the area around the junction of the Missouri and Mississippi rivers. Not long after this they continued to Iowa, but after suffering a severe epidemic of smallpox in 1802, they settled in northeast Nebraska. In the winter the tribe lived in lodges that had thick mud walls to keep them warm. In the summer, however, they used lightweight tepees. The Omaha had a long series of wars with the Sioux Nation, but in 1854 they were forced to give up their lands and move to Dakota County, Nebraska. Although the tribe were given the rights to purchase their own lands as individuals in 1882, many chose instead to remain on the reservation.

Osage

The ancestors of the Osage tribe inhabited lands in the Ohio Valley, but by the end of the 1600s the tribe had moved to the region around the Osage River in Missouri. In 1802 the three divisions of the Osage numbered in total around 5,500 people. The Osage were an aggressive peoples who often conducted wars against other local tribes. They were typical Plains Indians, leading a semi-nomadic lifestyle centered on hunting game animals and gathering wild produce; they also cultivated a few crops. In 1810, the United States government forced the Osage to hand over their lands in Missouri, Arkansas, and Oklahoma. They were relocated on reservations in northcentral Oklahoma and southeastern Kansas. Since that time, these lands have been found to host extensive oilfields. This discovery has made the 10,000 or so surviving tribal members the richest of the native peoples in North America.

Oto

The Oto (also spelled Otoe), along with the Iowa and Missouri tribes, was once part of the Winnebago nation at which time they lived north of the Great Lakes. When the Oto left this area, the Missouri went with them, but they soon argued, and the two tribes went their separate ways thereafter. The Oto established a typical Plains Indian culture, but were not powerful enough to withstand attacks by other local tribes. They eventually moved south and settled near the mouth of the Platte River, where they joined forces with the Pawnee tribe. In the early 1880s they moved again and took up residence in Oklahoma.

PAWNEE

NOT-CHI-MI-NE

The Pawnee tribe formerly occupied lands in what is now Texas, but by the early 1540s they had moved to the region of the Platte River in southern Nebraska. They split into four separate groups in the early 1700s at which time their population was around 10,000 people. These were the Skidi or Wolf, Grand, Republican, and Tapage (or Noisy) bands. The tribe flourished during this period, and by 1750 they had taken over further territories that extended as far as the Republican River in North Kansas and the Niobrara River in north Nebraska.

Their culture was typical of the Plains Indians. Uniquely, they also had a unusual set of myths and rituals. Part of these was the regular sacrifice of a young woman, but this practice had ended by the early 1800s. The Pawnee were fierce warriors who fought constantly with the Sioux and the Cheyenne, yet they formed close associations with the Oto. Their behavior was atypical in that they never fought against the United States government, even when badly provoked. Many Pawnee warriors became scouts for the U.S. Army or worked for the Union Pacific Railroad as guardians against attack by other tribes. Their population was greatly reduced by the combination of wars and epidemics of cholera and smallpox in the 1830s and 1840s. They gave up their lands in Nebraska and moved to a reservation in Oklahoma in 1876.

Pawnee. 3.

ND-TIN
A CHIPPEWA CHIEF

The Piegan tribe is one of the three tribes that formed the Blackfoot or Blackfeet confederacy. The other two were the North Blackfoot (Siksika) and the Blood (Kainah). The Piegan people were also known as the Pikuni. The name sometimes appears as Peigan (with the "e" and the "i" reversed) in Canada. An Algonkian people, they had a close alliance with the Atsina (or Gros Ventre) and Sarsi.

THESE POLES
ARE
RESPECTFULLY DEDICATED
TO OUR
TSESHAHT LEADERS
PAST, PRESENT AND FUTURE

WO-HAY-KE-GUO-GA

The Plains Cree called themselves Nehiawak, a term that cannot be etymologized. In 1640 and in reports for the next 20 years, the tribe was referred to as the Kinstinon by priests who had yet to meet any tribesmen, but learned from other Indians that the Cree were a very powerful people. Aside from being nomadic hunters, the Jesuits learned that the Cree fought the Nadouessis and Dakota. From 1656 to 1658, four geographical subdivisions of the Cree were named. The geographical boundaries were Lake Nipigon, west of James Bay, between Lake Nipigon and Moose River, and along the East Main River. This is consistent with the eastern Cree boundaries outlined in 1656, as defined by Skinner, who visited them some 250 years later.

PLAINS OJIBWA

According to their oral tradition, the Ojibwa originally emigrated from the region of the St. Lawrence River in the east along with the related Ottawa and Potawatomi peoples. The three tribes separated at what is now Mackinaw City, Michigan, and the Ojibwa spread west over a vast area along the shores of Lake Superior while the two other tribes settled to the south. The Ojibwa, Ottawa, and Potawatomi remained allies through much of their history, united in the Council of Three Fires.

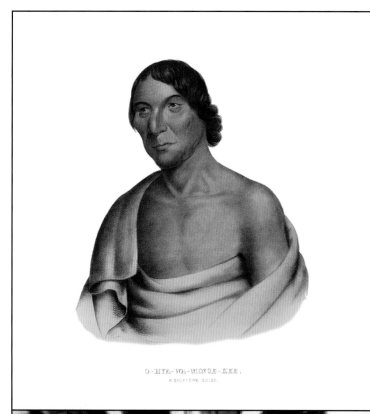

O-HYA-WA-MINCE-KEE.
A CHIPPEWA CHIEF.

The Salishan tribes are a linguistic family that inhabited the north portions of Washington state, northern Idaho, western Montana, and a small strip of the northwest coast of Oregon in the United States as well as the southeast part of Vancouver Island from Thurlow Island to Sooke Bay and all the south mainland of British Columbia as far as Bute inlet and Quesnelle Lake in Canada. An isolated division of the family, the Bellacoola, had established itself farther north on the Dean Inlet, Burke Channel, and Bellacoola River. The name Salish was originally applied to a large tribe in west Montana popularly known as Flatheads, and it was finally extended to cover all those speaking a similar language.

Sarsi

OKEE-MAKEE-QUID

The Sarsi (also spelled Sarcee) were a hunter-gatherer tribe that occupied lands on the upper Saskatchewan River in the early 1800s. Their language belonged to the Athabascan branch of the Nadene linguistic family. The small population of the Sarsi tribe left them vulnerable to attacks by the Cree and other tribes, so they formed an alliance with the Blackfoot people to gain the protection they needed. In 1877 the Canadian government managed to persuade them to give up their lands, and in 1880, they moved to a reservation located in Calgary, Alberta. In the early 1990s, the Sarsi people numbered around 800 individuals.

SIOUX (Teton/Yankatonai)

The Sioux people were a large confederation of native tribes who formerly occupied extensive homelands. A large part of these were distributed from the west bank of the Mississippi River northward from the Arkansas River almost as far as the Rocky Mountains, although not all of this area was open to them because it was also home to other tribes. The Northern Sioux lands reached well into Canada, and others lived in the Carolinas, Virginia, and in Mississippi along the Gulf coast. There were three major groupings of Sioux tribes: the Santee, or Eastern division, also known as the Dakota; the Nakota, or Middle division; and Lakota the Western division. The name Sioux is derived from the Chippewa name for this tribe, which translates as "snake" or "enemy." The Sioux were hostile to the large numbers of white settlers who came to their lands. As was the fate of all Native Americans, the Sioux tribes were forced onto reservations. Today their population is over 40,000.

SIOUX (TETON/YANKATONAI)

Sioux (Teton/Yankatonai)

O-IT-DE-WAH.
A CHIPPEWA CHIEF.

The Wichita (also spelled Witchita) were a small agricultural tribe whose ancestors are believed to come from Arkansas and Louisiana. Over the years they have lived on lands from central Texas to the Arkansas River. When the Spanish explorers encountered the Wichita, they were said to have lived in "houses made from grass." This was, in fact, an accurate description because the Wichita built their houses from a domed pole framework with an overlay of thatched grass. They refer to themselves as Kitikitish, which translates as "racoon eyelids." This name probably comes from the fact that the men used to tattoo lines on their eyelids. The name Wichita is most likely to come from the tribe's own word "wits" meaning "men." Although the tribe was forced out of Texas by white settlers, they never went to war against the United States. In 1850, they settled on a reservation in southern Oklahoma, but during the American Civil War they had to flee the area to avoid the widespread hostilities. They returned home soon after peace was declared. Today there are barely more than 300 living members of the tribe.

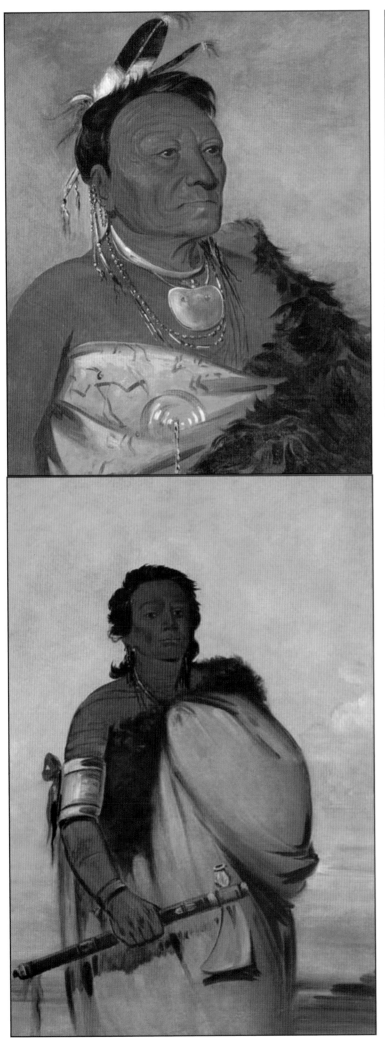

SOUTHWEST (INCLUDING PUEBLOS)

SACRED BUCKSKIN - APACHE

The Southwestern culture area is composed of the present day states of Arizona, New Mexico, and parts of southern Colorado and Utah, as well as adjoining parts of Mexico and Texas. There are three sub-regions: the northern area formed by Colorado, northern Arizona, and northern New Mexico; the western area, which runs along the border between Arizona and California; and the southern area that comprises southern Arizona, southern New Mexico, and adjacent areas of Mexico.

The region's local environments are dictated by the amount of rainfall they receive. In the more humid areas evergreen trees flourish, and in the drier areas Piñon pine and juniper predominate. The vegetation in the driest places is mostly scrub, cactus, and mesquite.

One of the region's earliest group of inhabitants was a semi-nomadic civilization called the Basket Makers. These people were originally primitive hunters. They used a prehistoric weapon called the atlatl to hunt their prey. The atlatl is a simple throwing device that allows a hunter to send a spear further and faster than is possible by hand alone. Using such weapons the Southwest tribes were able to bring down large animals such as bison or deer.

About 3,000 years ago, they started cultivating basic crops such as squash and beans. It is likely that these skills were learned from other local tribes. They also acquired the skills to make pottery, as well as the necessary knowledge to weave objects such as baskets and bags. As they became more familiar with these practices, they got better at them, and around 2,700 years ago their agricultural endeavors increased in productivity. They also started using the bow and arrow, which quickly made the atlatl obsolete. The Basket Makers built houses that were dug into the ground and lined with slabs of stone.

As the region dried out around 2,500 years ago, it could no longer support most of the game animals that previously lived there. As a result, the native peoples of the area were unable to survive by hunting alone. Those that were unwilling or unable to adapt moved away in search of more productive lands. The tribes that remained developed either predominantly agrarian or nomadic lifestyles. It was around this time that the ancestors of the Pueblo Indians settled in the region.

The name Pueblo is used to refer to any native tribe that lived in the Pueblo-style houses and does not indicate any specific tribe. These people brought with them a lot of new architectural and agricultural techniques. Their settlements were usually large communal affairs made from stone or adobe, which were often built partly underground. They typically had several floors or levels that were interconnected by ladders.

The land that was previously unforgiving was able to support these large communities because the new settlers built complicated irrigation systems to water the fields. One of the methods they employed was to construct large storage ditches to catch any rainwater that fell. This meant that their agricultural fields produced more than without benefit of irrigation and could therefore feed many more people. This success did not go unnoticed by other tribes in the region, and many of the nomadic tribes habitually raided the Pueblo Indians and stole their crops. These wandering tribes were used to gathering whatever they could obtain, and the Pueblo's fields of crops must have presented a tempting target to them. Most of the nomads lived in brush-covered wickiups that could be built quickly and easily as they moved from area to area in search of food.

The many native peoples of the Southwest region can be divided into five main categories: the agrarian Pueblo Indians, the Yuman-speaking tribes, the northern nomadic hunter-gatherers, the southwestern nomadic hunter-gatherers, and the various Mexican peoples. The Yuman-speaking tribes included the Havasupai, Hualapai, Yavapai, Mohave, Yuma, Cocopah, Maricopa, Pima, and Papago peoples. The nomadic hunter-gatherers from the north included the Apache and Navajo, and those from the southwest included the Karankawa and Coahuiltec. Although there were a great many different tribes in the area, the predominant language was the Uto-Aztecan branch of the Aztec-Tanoan linguistic stock.

The Apache are a large group of associated Native American tribes. The name Apache is thought to be from a Zuni word for "enemy" and so does not refer to any one specific people. In all there were around 40 or more different groups who were considered to be Apaches including the Chiricahua Apache, Coyotero, Jicarilla, Kiowa Apache, Lipan, Mescalero, Navaho, Western Apache, and White Mountain Apache. Some of these groups have since become assimilated into other native tribes.

It is thought that the Apache's ancestors came to the Southwest region around the year 1100 AD. Most subsisted on a mixture of hunting wild game and gathering foods such as cactus fruits and the seeds of wild shrubs and grasses. They often practiced some small-scale farming but would also regularly plunder grain from other tribes. The Apache were renowned for their warrior ways. The Eastern Apache were driven from their lands by the Comanche in the early 1720s. The main Apache territories were originally part of Mexico, but once they were acquired by the United States in the mid-1800s, confrontations with white settlers became commonplace.

The Apache are still a large group, with over 50,000 living on their extensive reservations in Arizona and New Mexico. Although they retain many of their original cultural practices, they have also managed to adapt to modern business ways and now run successful ranches, timber companies, mineral resource developments, and are also involved with tourism.

DAP PA TON SA
CHIEF OF THE DWARFS

The name Dieguéños is not that of a single tribe, but rather a Spanish term that refers to the Native Americans of the San Diego region in California. They generally wore little or no clothing, but instead wore highly decorative face and body paint. Jewelery was usually worn in the form of bead necklaces, stone or pottery pendants, and hair ornaments. They moved around through the year, but were not nomads because they followed well-organized routes between places where they owned land. They would travel to a location to take advantage of the best growing season then move on to the next site. They practiced advanced land management techniques, including controlled burning to reduce the risk from major bush fires and also used fertilizers to keep the soil in its best condition. They did not rely entirely on agriculture for their food supply, however. They also hunted small animals such as rabbits. Some of the original peoples from this group still live in the area, with about 400 officially recognized as Mission Indians.

HAVASUPAI

HO-PO-ETH-LE-YO-HO-LO.

The Havasupai are a tribe of Native Americans who live deep in the Havasu Canyon, which is in the northeast part of the Grand Canyon. They are descended from a Yuma tribe that lived in the canyon more than 1,000 years ago. The name breaks down as "Ha," meaning water; "Vasu," meaning blue; and "Pai," meaning people. This refers to the large waterfalls and blue waters that are natural features of their homeland. The Havasupai created effective irrigation systems, which helped them grow a bounty of crops that was the mainstay of their foodstuffs. Their culture dictated that the land itself was sacred because of its critical role in the tribe's survival. The tribal village was only accessible on horseback or by foot along narrow trails, making their homeland easy to defend. The women became expert basket weavers, a craft they still practice today using cottonwood and willow. There are about 640 Havasupai living today.

HOPI

The Hopi are a group of Pueblo Indians who were originally called Moki or Moqui. They were nonmigratory farmers who grow the usual native crops of corn, beans, and squash. They also grew fields of wheat, cotton, and tobacco and herded sheep. They inhabited several mesa villages in northeast Arizona, each of which was governed by a chief who also acted as the spiritual leader. The relative isolation of the Hopi meant that they did not have much contact with European settlers until comparatively recently. As a result, they did not suffer many of the problems that other tribes experienced during the period of white settlement. They did have problems with other Native Americans, however, and were often subjected to attacks by other tribes, especially the Navaho, during the 1700s and 1800s. The violence ended when the U.S. Army stepped in. Even though the Hopi were given a reservation of their own, the Navaho continued to move onto their lands. This is still an ongoing situation, although today the fighting tends to be restricted to the courts. Today the Hopi tribe has around 6,700 living members.

KERES

PADDY CARR.

The Keres are a group of Pueblo Indians who originally inhabited settlements along the Rio Grande in northcentral New Mexico. The Keres are one of four tribes of Eastern Pueblo Indians: the Keres, Tewa, Tiwa, and Towa. Their homes were carved into the cliffs composed of soft volcanic rock called tufa. When the Spanish first explored the area in 1540, they reported that the Keres were distributed across seven Pueblo settlements. A hundred years later it was estimated that they numbered around 4,000. Some of the settlements, such as the Pueblo of Zia, have been inhabited continuously since around the mid-1200s.

MARICOPA

PA-SHE-NINE
A CHIPPEWA CHIEF

The Maricopa are a Yuman tribe that since the 1800s has lived in the region of the Gila River in south Arizona. It is believed that they originally came from the Gulf of California area. Their name comes from the Pima people, whereas they refer to themselves as Pipatsje, which means "people."

Originally there were two groups of Pima: the Lower Pima and Upper Pima. Both lived in domed huts made from pole frames covered with mud and twigs. They were primarily farmers, but were also expert archers and also used war clubs and rawhide shields. Although the Pima had many problems with neighboring tribes, they were friendly toward white settlers, and their villages became regular resting places for pioneers making the long journey to California.

The Maricopa joined with the Pima tribe in the mid-1800s to help each other withstand attacks by the Yuma tribe, their mutual enemies. This alliance helped them win a spectacular victory against an attack in 1857 by a band of Yuma, Mohave, and Yavapai, when 90 of 93 Yuma warriors were killed. Shortly thereafter, the Papago tribe, who were closely related to the Pima, joined with them. The Papago had also been suffering badly from attacks by other tribes, in this case by the local Apaches. With help from the Papago and the Maricopa-Pima alliance, the U.S. government was able to broker a peace settlement on these violent neighbors.

The Maricopa, Pima, and Papago tribes shared a similar culture of farming and gathering foodstuffs from the wild, including mesquite beans and cactus fruit. The women were especially accomplished basket weavers. In 1859, a reservation was created for them on the Gila River, and another was later created on the Salt River. Today many members of the tribes are successfully involved in cattle ranching.

MOHAVE

In the mid-1800s, the Mohave inhabited lands on both banks of the Colorado River in Arizona and California, at which time their population was around 3,000. When the Spanish explorers arrived in the 1500s looking for gold, the Mohave, who were skilled potters, had the largest settlements in the region with each village divided into separate clans. The people, who generally had lots of tattoos, wore very little in the way of clothing. The men usually went about naked, and the women wore small cloths made from rabbit skins.

They were fierce warriors when necessary and traveled vast distances as peaceful traders, exchanging surplus crops for valued items. When they visited the native coastal tribes, for instance, they usually brought back seashells. Although the Mohave were initially friendly toward the first white fur trappers, they were appalled at the lack of respect the trappers demonstrated for the animals they killed. The trappers also failed to understand that the creatures they caught were considered Mohave property and taking them without payment was viewed as theft. Consequently, relations soon turned from amicable to extremely violent, and many people were killed on both sides.

In March 1865, the Colorado River Indian Reservation was created by the U.S. government near the southern range of the Mojave lands. Although several hundred people agreed to move to the area, others felt that the lands were too poor to farm and remained behind. They became known as the Fort Mohave tribe. A second reservation was eventually granted for them to live on. Most of the surviving members now live on the Colorado River Reservation.

PEE-CHE-KIR.
A CHIPPEWA CHIEF

The Navaho were one of the tribes known as the Apache, although they called themselves the D_né. The word Navaho comes from the Tewa people and refers to the large tracts of lands the Navaho occupied. Their homelands were arid areas with an average altitude of around 6,000 feet above sea level. The Navaho were relentless enemies of the Pueblo people and local white settlers in New Mexico, who they constantly raided. In order to stop these attacks, the U.S. Army invaded the Navaho lands and killed most of their sheep, rendering them unable to feed themselves The Army also took large numbers of the tribe as prisoners. The goal was to demonstrate to the Navaho that they should stop their aggression or face the consequences. In the end the prisoners were released, and they were given replacement stocks of sheep. The concept worked, and the Navaho not only remained peaceful, but their farms prospered. They were also very good weavers, and their blankets are still especially highly regarded. The Navaho now occupy a reservation of over 9.5 million acres in northeast Arizona, northwest New Mexico, and southeast Utah. Although these lands are not suited to horticulture, they are good for raising cattle, and as a result the tribe's primary income these days is from ranching.

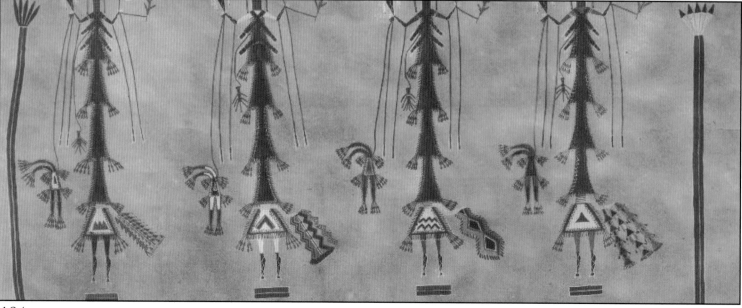

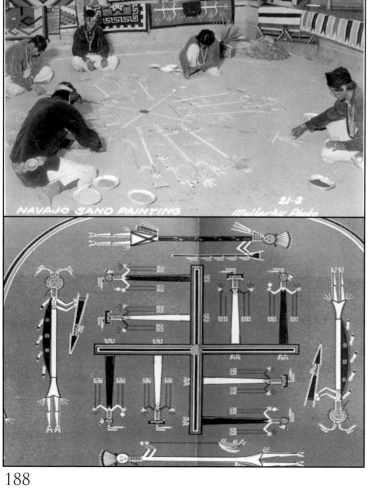

NAVAJO SAND PAINTING

21·3

Mullarky Photo

PAPAGO

Part of the Upper Piman tribes of south Arizona and north Mexico, the Papago have been Christians since 1687, quickly learning Spanish and then—after the transfer of their territory from Mexico to the U.S.—American ways. They still live in the area in sizeable numbers.

Pima

PETALESHAROO

A PAWNEE BRAVE

The Pima, who now prefer the name O'otain, are closely related to the Papago and are part of an old culture that developed canals for irrigation and a successful agricultural life. The Spanish brought livestock, wheat, and Catholicism. Today the O'otain live on reservations around the Gila and Salt rivers.

PUEBLO DWELLERS

Pueblo refers to any native tribe that lived in pueblo-style houses. A pueblo, or adobe, house is a modular, multi-story house made of adobe (clay and straw baked into hard bricks) or of large stones cemented together with adobe. Each adobe unit is home to one family, like a modern apartment. The whole structure, which can contain dozens of units, is often home to an entire extended clan.

The agrarian Pueblo Indians are the Hopi and Zuni tribes on the western side of the Rio Grande River, and the Keres, Tewa, Tiwa, Towa, and Piro on the eastern side. The Hopi Indians built their pueblos from stone and rendered them with clay on both the inside and outside. Their houses had no doors or windows, and could only be entered by climbing through a hole in the roof. The inhabitants dried their corn on the roofs of their houses before grinding it into a flour-like meal used extensively in their cooking. The women made clay bowls and the men wove cloth textiles.

The Anasazi Indians built their pueblos onto the sides of cliffs. Their pueblos were built of stone blocks held together with a mud-based mortar. Some had over 200 rooms and could house more than 400 people. Once the inhabitants had climbed into their homes by ladder, the ladders were pulled up, providing a degree of protection. Some of the rooms were purely for use by a single family, whereas others were communal. One such room was known as the kiva, an underground room, circular in shape and decorated with paintings of gods. It was exclusively for the use of men, who practiced various religious rituals there. It had no doors and could only be accessed by climbing a ladder through a hole in the ceiling.

The descendants of this population cultivated corn, beans, squash, cotton, and tobacco, also trading textiles woven from cotton and yucca fibers for buffalo meat from local hunter tribes. Along with growing crops, the Anasazi also made fine pottery.

POW - A - SHEEK

The Tewa are one of the group of four Eastern Pueblo tribes that live in the region of the Rio Grande in northern New Mexico and northeastern Arizona. They speak languages from the Tanoan linguistic family. The name Tewa comes from the Keres and translates as "moccasins." In the 1600s missionaries reported that about 6,000 Tewa people were living in eight pueblo settlements. Each one of the communities developed its own identifiable style of artwork that was incorporated into basket and textile weaving. The women tended to make the baskets, while the men wove the blankets, rugs, and fabrics.

The Tiwa (also spelled Tigua, Tiguex and Tihua) are a group of Native Americans who originally inhabited lands around Isleta, New Mexico, near what is now Albuquerque. They now live in the region of the Ysleta del Sur Pueblo near El Paso, Texas. When the Spanish explorers first reached the Tiwa, they were living in 13 or more settlements. At least three of these contained 200 or more individual houses, and it was estimated that the overall population was around 2,000. Although they were granted lands by the Spanish and Mexican governments - grants which were ratified by the State of Texas, they were still swindled out of their lands by unscrupulous property dealers by the late 1800s. The Tiwa were officially recognised as a tribe in 1967, and put under the jurisdiction of the Commission of Indian Affairs. The surviving members of the tribe currently number around 1,500, some of whom are attempting taking court action to title to some of their traditional lands.

WALAPAI (HUALAPAI)

QUA TA WA PAI
COL. LEWIS.

The Walapai were a small Yuman tribe that formerly lived in the region of the middle Colorado river. They were hunter-gatherers, who collected fruits, nuts and berries and hunted game. Their name translates as "Pine Tree Folk." The tribe has a reputation for being a hard-working and brave people. The Havasupai were an offshoot of the Walapai, and their languages are closely related. They fell foul of the American authorities in 1866 as a result of hostilities with local white settlers, and as a result were interned on the Colorado River reservation. Eventually they returned to their old lands and were assigned a reservation there. In 1910, the tribe numbered around 500 people and owned approximately 2,000 horses. Today about 1,500 Walapai survive, many of whom still live on their reservation.

KANT CHE WAI ME
FEMALE FLYING PIGEON

The Yuma originally lived where the Gila and Colorado rivers met in southwestern Arizona. They were hunter-gatherers who also grew crops of corn, pumpkin, and beans. The Yuma language family was divided into two distinct groups: the River Yumas, which included the Cocopa, Hakchidhoma, Maricopa, Mojaves, and Yuma; and the Upland Yumas, which included the Walapai, Havasupai, and Yavapai. The United States government assigned the Fort Yuma Indian Reservation to the tribe in 1884. Today there are about 3,000 living members of the tribe.

ZUÑI

The Zuni were a farming people known for their craftsmanship skills in basketry, weaving, pottery, and jewelery. Their hand-made products featured elaborate designs, including many different animal motifs. Early Spanish explorers attacked and ransacked the Zuni villages, erroneously believing that they had large amounts of gold hidden away. This misconception was as a result of the Spanish trying to locate legendary places that were said to be filled with treasure. The Zuni also suffered from attacks by the local Navaho and Apache Indians for many years. Their present day reservations are in McKinley County in western New Mexico, and their population numbers around 9,000.

SOUTHEAST

The Southeast culture area stretches from the Ohio River to the Gulf of Mexico and includes parts of Arkansas, Kentucky, Missouri, Oklahoma, Tennessee, Texas, Maryland, Virginia, West Virginia, North Carolina, South Carolina, Florida, George, Alabama, Louisiana, and Mississippi.

Most of the region has fertile soil and good rainfall so that many forests grow in the area. The trees are mostly southern yellow pine, a species that thrives in the mild, wet climate, although cypress also does well. The coast is lined in saltwater marshes, the most extensive of which is the Everglades in Florida. Mountain ranges stretch like a spine through the center of the region and include the Blue Ridge, Smoky, and Cumberland Mountain ranges, which are all part of the Appalachians.

The early inhabitants of the region, before 500 AD, were semi-nomads who lived a hunter-gatherer lifestyle. They were opportunists who hunted animals with the bow and arrow or with a blowpipe. They fished by poisoning streams or with simple traps, also collected berries, fruit, roots, or shellfish depending on what was available at the time. From 500 AD to 900 AD, they began to settle and establish themselves as farmers. From 900 AD to 1100 AD they began to make pottery and build burial mounds, also taking up tobacco smoking and trading on a large scale with other tribes.

The villages they built were mostly sited along the river valleys where there was shelter and the land was more fertile. Most of their houses were built from wattle and daub, a process in which strips of wood or thin poles are made into a framework and covered with a mixture of mud and straw. The roofs were made from a variety of different materials, including bark, grass thatch, bamboo, palm fronds, or animal hides.

They became adept at growing crops of various kinds of beans, as well as squash, pumpkins, and sunflower seeds. The typical pattern was for the men to clear the land and for the women to plant and tend the crops. At other times the men would hunt and the women would gather whatever was available. Once the soil was exhausted by having too many crops grown on it, the villages would be relocated to a fresh position.

Many of the tribes lived warlike existences. In order to defend themselves they encircled their villages with strong wood and earthen fences called palisades. It was common practice for warriors to be tattooed with symbols representing their particular exploits, and many battles were purely for the purposes of glorification, rather than for any specific military reason. The settlements usually had religious structures where elaborate ceremonies would be carried out before and after significant battles, both to ask for blessings and to thank the spirits for their assistance.

At more peaceful times other complicated rituals such as sun worship were practiced. These rituals usually involved raising spirits, the consumption of

TAH-CHEE
A CHEROKEE CHIEF.

special substances with medicinal powers, and much dancing. Burial ceremonies were especially highly regarded, and great efforts were made to honor their ancestors in the process. Certain objects, such as pottery, were often included in the burial mounds. These buried items are known as grave goods and were believed to help the deceased more easily traverse the journey into the afterlife—similar to the items buried with the dead in the Egyptian culture. Harvest ceremonies, in which thanks were given to the spirit world for a good harvest, were considered to have especial relevance. These ceremonies often lasted for several days. The most important part of the ceremony for many tribes was known as the green corn dance.

The native peoples of the region wore clothes made from several sources. Deerskin was popular for shirts, breechcloths, dresses, and leggings. Textiles were also made by weaving together beaten plant fibers or by sewing turkey feathers over a network of twisted fibers. The clothes they made were often highly decorated. They also wore body paint to enhance their tattoos.

The social structures of the Southeast tribal villages were complicated and well organized. Most had a chief, who was usually male. He could be head of a single village, a group of villages, or the whole tribe. Each chief would take counsel from several advisors, who were elder members, shamans, or assistants. The Natchez tribe had a form of nobility with a strong hierarchy; the king was referred to as the "Great Sun" and his family was known as the "Suns." Below the king in the hierarchy were the Nobles and Honored Men and Women, and the lowest class were the commoners.

When the European settlers arrived, the area was soon overrun by every sort of person, from traders to gold prospectors. Some of the traders were slavers and sent most of their unfortunate captives back to Europe to work for those who could afford them. Other traders exchanged tools and various utilitarian items for buffalo hides and agricultural produce. Missionaries traveled throughout the area, seeking to convert the natives to Christianity.

Many of the settlers got on well with the natives, while others came into conflict with them. This was especially true where land was concerned. Many disputes escalated into small-scale wars, and people were killed on both sides. As in the other culture areas, the biggest killer of Native Americans was disease; smallpox and measles were especially virulent in the Southeast region.

After the Revolutionary War, several of the Southeast tribes understood that the Europeans were there to stay, and as a means of survival and acclimation to their new environment chose to adopt their ways. These tribes became known as the Five Civilized Tribes," comprising the Cherokee, Creek, Choctaw, Chickasaw, and Seminole. They wore European clothes and learned to speak English.

After the Indian Removal Act was instituted in 1830 most of the tribes in the Southeast region were relocated to the Indian Territories in what is today the state of Oklahoma. Thousands of natives died during the move. Some were taken by transport, while others were forced to march. This infamous journey became known by the Cherokee as The Trail of Tears, a term that was later used to refer to many other native relocations. Some small groups were able to avoid the authorities by hiding in the mountains of eastern Tennessee and western North Carolina.

Many different languages were spoken in the region. Some were even specific to individual villages. They include the Atakapan, Nathesan, Yuchian and Chitimachan languages. Although today the remaining tribal members have adopted most modern ways, many are doing their best to ensure that their tribal traditions are not forgotten. Many tribal children are being taught the ways of their ancestors as part of their education, and this will hopefully foster sufficient interest for this important knowledge to stay alive.

The Alabama-Coushatta were two separate tribes that now share a reservation in Texas. The state of Alabama was named after the Alabama tribe. Before moving to west Louisiana and eastern Texas in the 19th century, they inhabited lands in southern Alabama, where they were members of the Creek Confederacy. They speak a language that belongs to the Muskogean branch of the Hokan-Siouan linguistic stock.

APALACHEE

SE QUO YA

The Apalachee tribe were successful farmers on the Florida panhandle from the Aucilla River westward, an area known as Apalachee Bay. The land they grew their crops on was extremely fertile and under their skilled hands it was very productive. This fortunate circumstance allowed their settlements to prosper and the population to expand. At its peak, the tribe probably numbered 5,000 members. Apalachee is likely a Choctaw word for "people on the other side." This warlike tribe initially sided with the Spanish and thus suffered defeat at the hands of the British. Over 1,000 Apalachees were captured and sold as slaves. Further troubles led to the tribe more or less disappearing in the 1800s.

SHA HA KA
A MANDAN CHIEF.

The Biloxi have always lived on the fertile lands along the Mississippi River in what are today Mississippi and Louisiana. In the late 17th century, the Tunica tribe first encountered French explorers, who claimed the Indians' homeland for their king. The Tunica soon became valuable long-term allies of French colonists who settled nearby in the 1700s. After Great Britain forced France to abandon its North American colonies in the 1760s, the Tunica came under control of England, then Spain, and finally the United States.

CALUSA

The Calusa Indians were descended from some of the earliest inhabitants of North America who moved into southwest Florida around 12,000 years ago. Then the climate was much colder, and hardwood forests flourished. Many kinds of large animals were common, including woolly mammoths, sabre-toothed tigers, and giant sloths. At one time, the tribe was called the Calos, which translates as "the fierce people." Hunter-gatherers, the Calusa were nevertheless not typical nomadic peoples. Instead they evolved a complex culture that included strong political structures and well-developed art forms.

As the climate became warmer, the seas were more welcoming and they could depend less on hunting large land animals. The Calusa's use of the sea is reflected in the fact that they are also known as the Shell People. They used shells to make all manner of things, from weapons to tools and jewelery. As a people they were very tall, often up to four inches taller than their European counterparts and usually had long hair. The Calusa had good sailing skills and carved canoes from tree trunks. The tribe itself died out in the 1800s, mostly as a result of exposure to diseases like smallpox.

The Catawba tribe formerly occupied part of South Carolina. They were a large and aggressive people who waged a long series of wars against the Cherokee and other local tribes. These efforts were essentially unsuccessful, and combined with several epidemics of smallpox, reduced their numbers considerably. By the end of the 18th century the Catawba were a very small group. Their language belongs to the Siouan branch of the Hokan-Siouan linguistic family. Some surviving members still live in and around the South Carolina.

The Cherokee tribe played an important part in the history of the United States. As a result they are one of the better-known Native American groups. It is believed that they originally came from the northern Mexico or Texas region, and at some stage they migrated up to the Great Lakes area. They were then forced out of these lands by wars with the Iroquois and Delaware tribes, and finally settled in the regions of the Allegheny and Appalachian mountains in North and South Carolina, Tennessee, north Georgia, and Alabama.

Their first exposure to Europeans was the Spanish explorers who encountered them in 1540. Although they lost a large proportion of their population to a massive smallpox epidemic in 1715, their numbers slowly recovered and they are now one of the largest Native American tribes in the United States. In the late 18th and early 19th centuries, many thousand Cherokee members moved to lands west of the Mississippi River; this group is known as the Western Band.

CHICKASAW (CHIKASHA)

SPRING FROG
A CHEROKEE CHIEF.

The Chickasaw (also known as the Chikasha) are a tribe that formerly occupied lands in the northern Mississippi region. Although they were closely related to the Choctaw in both language and culture, they fought a long series of wars with them and were also engaged in on-and-off wars with the Creek, Cherokee, and Shawnee tribes. In the conflicts between Great Britain and France, the Chickasaw sided with the British. The French tried to make peace with the Chickasaw, but all attempts failed. After being severely weakened by endless conflicts and outbreaks of disease, the Chickasaw moved to Oklahoma under terms of a treaty and became one of the Five Civilized Tribes. Their language belongs to the Muskogean branch of the Hokan-Siouan linguistic family.

CHITIMACHA

STM. MA.NU.

The Chitimacha occupied lands in the delta region of the Mississippi River and the adjacent Atchafalaya Basin of southcentral Louisiana. Until the mid-1700s, they were considered to be the most powerful Native American tribe of the northern Gulf coast west of Florida. They fiercely contested attempts by the French to colonize Louisiana, battling with them for a long time. Nevertheless, their greatest population losses were due to the diseases brought by the French. It is estimated that in the 16th and 17th centuries, epidemics of smallpox, measles, and influenza killed close to half of the Chitimacha peoples.

They had a hunter-gatherer culture and benefited from the sea's enormous bounty. Their land was extremely fertile and the growing season was almost continuous. In addition, game animals were plentiful. Not having to travel or forage for food gave them time to develop a complex culture, which included the practice of cranial shaping to flatten their foreheads. They also became expert craftsmen and were particularly good at basket weaving. Although they had to relinquish large areas of their original territories to early European settlers, they are one of the few native groups from the Florida region that have managed to retain some of their ancestral lands to the present day. Most of the remaining members of the tribe live on or close to the Chitimacha reservation at Charenton, Louisiana.

The main proportion of the Choctaw tribe originally occupied lands in central and southern Mississippi, although there were other smaller groups in Alabama, Georgia, and Louisiana. They were very skilled farmers, with a culture that was closely related to those of the Creek and Chickasaw, even though these tribes were their long-term enemies. In the war between Britain and France over ownership of the North American continent, the Choctaw aligned themselves with the French colonists, and thus fared badly when the British won the war. In 1832, the Choctaw were forced to hand over their Alabama and Mississippi lands. They moved to the Indian Territories in Oklahoma, where they became established as one of the Five Civilized Tribes.

CREEK OR MUSKOGEE

The Creek are a confederacy of Native American Indians who originally lived in Alabama and Georgia. They were nonmigratory farmers who often settled along rivers and creeks, and it was for this habit that European traders named them. The Creek Confederacy was formed as an alliance of the inhabitants of about 50 small towns across the region against incursions by aggressive northern tribes. The Creek tribesmen were recognized by early European explorers as being tall, proud people who loved to decorate themselves with all manner of ornaments. Although they were initially friendly toward the British, in part because of their hostility toward the Spanish, in 1813 they rose up against the British in the Creek War. After they were defeated at the battle of Horseshoe Bend, they were forced to cede two-thirds of their lands to the United States government. In the end they moved to the Indian Territories in Oklahoma, where they became established as one of the Five Civilized Tribes. Today more than 20,000 Creek Indians still live in Oklahoma.

KADOHADACHO OR CADDO

The Caddo (also spelled Caddoe) or Kadohadacho are a Native American people who formerly inhabited territories across Louisiana, Texas, Arkansas, and Kansas. They were a nonmigratory tribe with strong religious beliefs that regimented their lives. They lived in small settlements in conical grass huts under a strong class system. Although they were primarily farmers, they were also accomplished horse breeders and traders. During the troubles caused by the arrival of European settlers and the complications that consequently arose, they formed a federation with several other local tribes. The other tribes in this loose alliance included the Arikara, Pawnee, Wichita, and others, all of whom had similar cultures. The surviving members of the Caddo tribe now live on a reservation in Oklahoma.

NATCHEZ

The Natchez tribe was a people who lived along St. Catherine's Creek, east of the city of Natchez, Mississippi. They were the most powerful tribe in the lower Mississippi region. They were nonmigratory farmers who grew corn, beans, and squash and also hunted for buffalo and deer, rabbits and turkey. The Natchez were sun worshippers with a complex social structure and a class system based on marriage and ancestry. When a chief died, his wives, guards, and servants were killed by strangulation in order that they could accompany him in his journey to the afterlife. The Natchez had good relations with the French for many years, but war eventually broke out over land disputes. The French, helped by the Choctaw, heavily defeated the tribe and many of the Natchez survivors were sold into slavery. Some managed to avoid capture and settled among the Chickasaw, who were their allies. As a result, the tribe intermarried so much that by the beginning of the 20th century it had more or less disappeared as a distinct entity.

THAYENDANEGEA,
THE GREAT CAPTAIN OF THE SIX NATIONS

The state of Oklahoma has a particular significance to Native American Indians because many of them ended up in the government-appointed Indian Territories. When the first Europeans arrived as explorers, several tribes were already living there: the Osage, Kiowa, Arapaho, Wichita, and Caddo peoples. Most were hunter-gatherers who hunted buffalo when the opportunity arose, but of course this was prior to the horse, and farmed the land the rest of the time. They grew primarily corn, beans, and squash. The explorers, first arriving in the 16th century, were largely Spaniards in search of gold. The French, who claimed the land for their king, followed in the Spaniards footsteps. The French initially ventured into the region purely as explorers, but in the 1700s began to build trading posts to profit from furs and other products bought from Indian hunters.

In 1800, the area was given by the Spanish to the French, and then in 1803 it was sold to the United States in the Louisiana Purchase. Because the lands in the east were more desirable to the European settlers, the government had to move the Indians, and Oklahoma seemed ideal for the purpose. It was distant and not a desirable place for the Europeans to live, thus perfect for the Native Americans. Five tribes, many of whose members marched on foot, took the infamous journey known as the Trail of Tears. Close to 75,000 embarked, but many thousands died on the way from disease, hunger, and cold. The five tribes—the Seminoles, Creeks, Chickasaws, Choctaws, and Cherokees—came to be known as the Five Civilized Tribes.

OKMULGEE

The Okmulgee tribe formerly occupied lands in the region of the Chattahoochee River, Russell County, Alabama. The name comes from the Hitchiti language and means "where water boils up." This may well refer to the local natural features called Indian Springs in Butts County, Georgia. They were a small group at the best of times, but in the mid-1700s the Okmulgee only had 20 to 30 adult male members. By the early 1820s the tribe had grown to a total, including women and children, of about 220. The Okmulgee were closely associated with the nearby Chiaha and Osochi tribes. Their language came from the Muskhogean linguistic family.

SEMINOLE

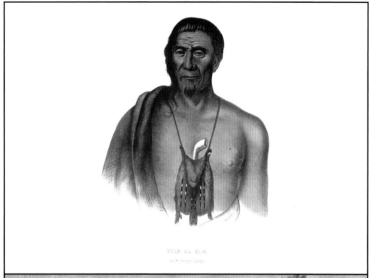

The Seminole was a group of affiliated Native American tribes who began banding together in the early 18th century to avoid white enslavement and land disputes and associated problems. Other tribes continued to join them until the beginning of the 19th century. They originated in Georgia, Alabama, and South Carolina, and finally settled in Spanish-held north and central Florida. The name is from the Muskogee word *simano-li,* which means "runaway."

When the United States government tried to take their new lands, they fought back in what became known as the First Seminole War. Eventually a treaty gave them lands east of Tampa Bay, but these were taken by the Payne's Landing Treaty of 1832. The tribe reacted angrily and started the Great Seminole War. After seven years of conflict and many thousands of deaths, the war finally came to an end in 1842. Although some members of the tribe were allowed to remain in Florida, most were removed to the Indian Territories in Oklahoma, where they became established as one of the Five Civilized Tribes. Today about 12,500 members of the tribe survive. Most still live in Oklahoma.

TAENSA

The Taensa (Taenso, Tahensa, Takensa, Tenisaw, Tenza, or Tinza) Indians were Muskhogean-speaking Indians who originally lived near the Mississippi River in northeast Louisiana. In the early 19th century, after they had moved to southwest Louisiana, the Taensas petitioned the Spanish government for lands in southeast Texas. They were granted permission to settle between the Trinity and Sabine rivers, but the move was never made.

TSHI-ZUN-HAU-KAU
A WINEBAGO.

The Tunica and Biloxi tribes settled long ago on the rich farming lands of the Mississippi River in what today are the states of Mississippi and Louisiana. They were hunter-gatherers who grew corn and squash and also collected many kinds of foods from the wild. The women gathered fruits, berries, seeds, and nuts, and also dug for various roots and tubers. The men hunted for game animals, especially deer and buffalo, from which they gained meat as well as hides and other important materials such as fat and sinew. Their villages were composed of round huts built from vertical posts through which canes were woven then rendered with clay and topped with thatched roofs. The huts themselves were situated around an open central area where feasts, dances, and games were held; a temple would normally be sited nearby. Religion played a strong part in the culture of these tribes, with the sun considered an important deity. Most of the Tunica and the Biloxi tribes joined together in the early 1800s, and several other local groups merged with them over the next few decades. In 1981, they were officially recognized by the United States government as the Tunica-Biloxi tribe.

NORTHEAST

The region that makes up the Northeast culture area comprises much of the North Atlantic coast. The southernmost point is just south of the Ohio river. The region stretches north as far as the temperate parts of southern Canada, then reaches inland across the Appalachian Mountains and as far west as the Mississippi River Valley. The Great Lakes mark the northern border in the interior, with Pennsylvania delineating the southern edge.

This large area contains many major rivers—including the St. Lawrence, Ohio, Wabash, Hudson, and Susquehanna—and lakes, especially those known as the Great Lakes. Almost all of the region is forested with mature trees, both coniferous and deciduous. Where the conifers proliferate wildlife is scarce, but the deciduous woodlands support all manner of suitable target animal species. The main focus was deer, which provided food in the form of meat as well as clothing and shelter that was made from skins and vitally important binding materials from sinew. The binding materials were used for making clothes, shoes, and most importantly, weapons.

Because finding enough food and shelter to survive was relatively straightforward in this region, many different tribes settled there. The archaeological remains suggest that the first native settlers arrived around 9,000 years ago.

Food sources were abundant, but they had to be searched for, so most of the tribes that settled in the region were semi-nomadic. They had permanent homes in large villages and also used temporary structures when they were away from the village hunting and/or gathering. They assembled these shelters from whatever brushwood was on hand at the time.

When they were away from their villages, the Algonquian-speaking tribes such as the Chippewa and

the Abenaki would gather nuts, berries, and wild grains while others hunted small animals such as deer or rabbits. The tribes that lived along the coast would also fish with spears, traps, hooks, and nets as well as gather shellfish along the shoreline. Fishing excursions were made more successful with the advent of the birch-bark canoe, which was lightweight and very maneuvrable, making them ideal for the task.

Some of the tribes people, generally the women, supplemented their food supplies by growing crops of corn, sunflowers, beans, and squash when the fields were suitably close to sources of fresh water. Many seed-bearing plants were farmed; the seeds were collected and stored for the next season's crop. The seeds were also ground into flour and made into bread or other foodstuffs. The cooking utensils were made of wood or simple black pottery.

The abundance of trees meant that there was always plenty of firewood for cooking and keeping warm, as well as for more structural purposes such as building shelters, be they temporary or permanent. Different tribes had different solutions to the issue of housing; some, such as the Iroquois, built substantial communal long houses with separate areas for each family. Often the long house would have several fireplaces and a series of smoke holes in the roof to allow the smoke to escape. The communal residential long houses of the Northeast region could be up to 50-feet long. Some tribes also built massive ceremonial long houses which could be up to 200-feet long and 30-feet high. The roofs and walls of these structures were generally made weather proof with large pieces of tree bark.

Most of the Algonquian groups, however, constructed villages of dome-shaped wigwams made of poles and covered with bark or skins, instead of long houses. In order to protect themselves against attack by enemies or animals such as bears and mountain lions, most villages were also surrounded by tall wooden fences made from sharpened poles up to 12-feet high.

For the native tribes in the region, the preferred choice of material for clothes was generally deerskin, because of its warmth, softness, and suppleness. The Indians used it to make leggings, shirts, breechcloths, and dresses. Many people also painted their faces, and the men often shaved both sides of their heads. Grease made from bear fat was commonly used to condition the hair.

Like most Native American Indians, the tribes people of the Northeast region were very spiritual. They believed a strong link existed between man and nature, and the sight of Europeans cutting down entire forests and killing large numbers of animals with no regard for the consequences upset them deeply. They perceived connections between the world around them and the spirits in more or less every aspect of daily life. Different tribes had different interpretations for how certain animals interacted with the spirits. It was thought that shamans, or medicine men, could summon helper spirits to aid them in curing diseases or bestowing good luck on hunting expeditions.

When the first European settlers arrived on the North Atlantic coast, the first natives they met were from the Northeast tribes. Many of these new arrivals had little or no idea as to how to survive, unbelievably they had not bothered to learn before they left to cross the ocean. Some of these people owed their lives to the local Native Americans who showed them how to grow crops and deal with other vital tasks. This positive association did not last, however, and before long disputes broke out over land ownership, often resulting in serious fighting.

When Britain and France started battling for control over North America, most of the tribes in the region fought for one side or the other. In many cases this meant that the native tribes were in conflict with each other, as well as with their European foes. The Iroquois League sided with the British, and this assistance meant the French were forced out of most of the region. The Huron and many Algonquian-speaking tribes, however, sided with the French. When the Revolutionary War broke out, the Iroquois League started to collapse as some groups sided with the British and others with the colonists. The league finally ended not long afterwards as a result of disease and other problems.

The Iroquois have managed to retain their ancestral lands, although many of the other tribes from the Northeast region are now located in Oklahoma and neighboring states as a result of U.S. government relocation.

The Abenaki tribe (also spelled Abnaki, Abanaki, Abinaki, and Abenaqui) occupied lands in what are now the states of Maine, New Hampshire, and Vermont, although their tribal legends suggest they originally came from the southwest. The tribe were hunter-gatherers who also grew crops, hunted, and fished depending on the season. They lived in small villages of conical huts surrounded by strong wooden fences. The Abenaki sided with the French in the Colonial Wars and as such fought the British for many years. When they were eventually defeated, they retreated into Canada, along with other related tribes. These included the Malecite, Passamaquoddy, Pennacook, and Penobscot, as well as various other smaller groups. The tribal name Abenaki was derived from Wabanaki or Wobanaki, an Indian word that translates as "those living at the sunrise."

The Algonquians (also spelled Algonkians, Algonquins, and Algonkins) were a small group of Native American Indians who formed alliances with the early French explorers and settlers. They fell foul of the Iroquois, against whom they were no match, and in the 1600s their tribe was fragmented across parts of southern Canada. It was more or less at this time that the tribe as an entity ceased to exist. Their language was part of the Algonquian-Wakashan linguistic family.

TUSTENNUGGEE EMATHLA

The Brothertown (also spelled Brotherton) were a group formed by Christian Indians from the areas of New England and Long Island, New York. The Christian religion became popular with several tribes including the Mohegan, Montauk, Narragansett, Niantic, Pequot, Tunxis, and Wangunk. This movement was part of the Great Awakening, which occurred during the 1740s in New England. As a consequence of their new-found sensibilities, they did their best to avoid the rampant alcoholism and other social problems that were rife amongst the settlements of North America. In the 1770s two Mohegan ministers led a large group of New England tribal families to new homelands in the territories of the Oneida tribe in northcentral New York. The name Brothertown was used because they wanted to live as Christian brothers.

Shortly afterward the Stockbridge tribe also moved to Oneida lands, and the pressures from European settlers did not abate. Their constant demand for new farmland meant the territories were badly eroded, leaving them with little option but to move to new territories where they would no longer be under threat. They chose to move to Wisconsin, and following the signing of the appropriate treaties, they bought most of the western shores of Lake Michigan. The move began in the early 1830s, but it was not long before ever increasing numbers of white settlers also moved to the area. They brought with them the very problems the Brothertown had been trying to leave behind.

Once the settlers realized that the area was good farmland, the Brothertown came under a lot of pressure to relinquish their lands. Many sold their farms and moved to other areas, which resulted in their becoming even more scattered over the next 100 years. Land disputes concerning their original homelands in New York and attempts to regain federal recognition for the tribe continue to this day. There are around 1,650 tribal members alive today.

CAYUGA

The Cayuga Nation are referred to by many different names, including the later term Seneca-Cayuga. The name Cayuga means the "people of the marsh." The name Seneca comes from the Iroquoian language and translates as "people of the standing rock," although they were also known as the "keepers of the Western door." The Cayuga moved to Ohio after the American Revolution, where they settled on a reservation along the Sandusky River. Both the Cayuga and the Seneca tribes banded together with others—the Conestoga, Mingo, Mohawk, Oneida, Onondaga, Shawnee, and Tuscarora—under the Iroquois Confederacy. Eventually the entire alliance moved to the Indian Territories in the State of Oklahoma. They experienced many problems as a result of border disputes, and during the American Civil War many battles were fought on their lands causing many to flee to safety elsewhere. Today most of the tribe's members still live in Oklahoma.

DELAWARE

WEE-TOP-K-NOT.

The Delaware peoples were not a single tribe, but an alliance of several closely associated tribes. In the 1600s they inhabited lands in the Delaware, New Jersey, eastern Pennsylvania, and southeastern New York areas. The name Delaware was applied to them by the English settlers, because they lived in the region of the Delaware River. They referred to themselves as Lenni-Lenape. The tribal alliance was based on three main groups: the Munsee, meaning "wolf"; the Unalachtigo, meaning "turkey"; and the Unami, meaning "turtle." In the early days, the Delaware peoples did a lot of trading with the Dutch. As land pressures developed, however, they sold much of their homeland and moved inland to the Susquehanna Valley. The Iroquois attacked them in 1720, and as a result they were forced to move again, this time to Ohio. After various troubles with the European settlers, they were defeated and had to hand over their lands once more. After traveling extensively, they were eventually moved to the Indian Territory where they settled with the Cherokee.

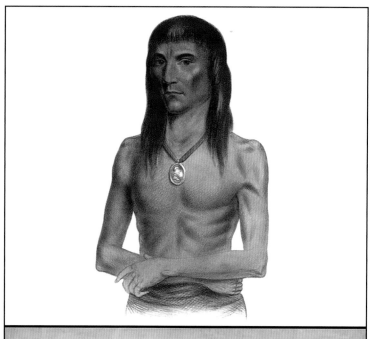

The Sac and the Fox tribes were close allies for many years. The Sac, who are sometimes referred to as the Sauk, lived as skilled farmers who participated in raiding parties against other tribes from time to time. The Fox, who are also known as the Mesquaki, were fierce warriors who waged a long-standing war against the Ojibwa. They originally occupied lands in the Saginaw Bay area in east Michigan, but as a result of their raiding parties were driven out of the region by the Ottawa and Neutral tribes. Both the Sac and the Fox moved north into what is now the state of Wisconsin. It was not long before they were at war with the French, as well as with the Sioux and the Illinois tribes. The French finally decided they had taken enough harassment and commenced to wipe out the Fox. This reduced their numbers to such an extent that they were no longer a significant force. It was at this time in the early 1730s that the Fox banded together with the Sac on a permanent basis. Since then, the two tribes have been known as the Sac and Fox. In the early and mid-1800s, their aggressive ways started the Black Hawk War, after which they were forced to move away. They wandered for some time and finally settled on reservations in Iowa, Kansas, and Oklahoma.

HURON OR WYANDOT

The Huron tribe were so named by early French explorers and settlers after the bristled haircuts worn by the warriors. The tribe called themselves the Wendat, an Iroquoian word that translates as "islanders" or "dwellers on a peninsula." When they weren't fighting, the tribal members were good farmers who grew the typical crops of the Native American Indians: corn, squash, and beans. They also cultivated tobacco and sunflowers in the fields around their palisaded villages.

In the 1600s the Huron fought a long war with the Iroquois that ended when an epidemic of malaria weakened the Huron and the Dutch armed the Iroquois with guns. The Huron were badly defeated and fled south to the Neutral Nation. Others went to the southwest to the Tobacco Nation or even north into Canada to seek protection from the French. This cost their new hosts dearly; the Iroquois invaded both the Neutral and Tobacco Nations, and more or less wiped them out. The survivors settled in Wisconsin and Illinois, where they fell foul of the Sioux. This forced them to move yet again to areas near Detroit, Michigan, and Sandusky, Ohio. Those who had taken refuge in Canada were given a small reservation to live on, where some still live to this day.

The Huron fought with the British in the American Revolution and in the War of 1812. The British called the tribe the Wyandotte or Wyandot. Although they had their lands confirmed by the government authorities, they sold them off and in 1842 moved to Kansas, in what is now called Wyandotte County. This was not a lasting solution, however, because white settlers kept usurping more and more of their lands. Finally, they bought some land from the Seneca Tribe in the Indian Territory in Oklahoma, where many of their approximately 3,600 descendants still live.

NA-ESI-BOESH-KAA

The Illini, also known as the Kaskaskia, were a federation of several Native American Indian tribes: the Cahokia, Kaskaskia, Michigamea, Moingwena, Peoria, and Tamaroa tribes. The name Peoria translates as "he comes carrying a pack on his back." In the 1600s, these peoples inhabited lands in south Wisconsin and north Illinois, as well as parts of Iowa and Missouri. At that time there were about 6,500 tribal members, but within 100 years, wars with the Sioux, Fox, and Iroquois reduced this figure to around 2,000. The situation worsened when a tribal member assassinated Pontiac, the famous chief of the Ottawa tribe. The Lake tribes blamed the Illini and a program of extermination began. By the end of the 18th century the Illini had only about 150 surviving members. In 1833, these last survivors sold their lands in Illinois and moved to a reservation in Miami County, Kansas. Today the descendants of these people live on a reservation in northeast Oklahoma that they purchased from the Quapaw and Shawnee tribes.

IROQUOIS

The Iroquois Confederacy, which was formed around the 14th century, was initially composed of five groups, hence the confederacy's title of Five Nations. The five tribes were the Cayuga and Oneida, known as the "Younger Brothers"; the Mohawk, called the "Eastern Doorkeepers"; the Onondaga, known as the "Firekeepers"; and the Seneca, known as the "Western Doorkeepers." They were later joined by the Tuscarora, who were accordingly titled the Adopted Brothers. The Iroquois had a sophisticated political system and were the most powerful Native American military force in North America. When the Huron pushed them too far, the Iroquois used Dutch guns to hunt them and their allies down however far they fled. These conquests included the Huron in 1649, the Tobacco and the Neutral Nations in 1650, the Erie in 1656, the Conestoga in 1675, and the Illinois around the year 1700. The borders of their territories were only formed due to the presence of other powerful tribes: to the west was the Ojibwa, to the south was the Cherokee and Catawba, and to the north was the French.

KICKAPOO

In the 1600s the Kickapoo (also spelled Kikapoo or Kikapu) inhabited lands in southwest Wisconsin. Although their culture was similar to that of Eastern Woodlands tribes—in other words an agricultural and gathering lifestyle—their location, which bordered the Plains Indians, meant that they also developed into accomplished buffalo hunters. When the Illini tribes incurred the wrath of the Kickapoo and their allies, the Ojibwa, Ottawa, Potawatomi, and Sac and Fox, the Illini were heavily defeated. Their lands were then divided up and the Kickapoo took over the region around central Illinois. They were later forced to relinquish these territories, when they traveled to Missouri and then on to Kansas. Many disliked the reservation they were assigned and moved to Mexico around 1852. In order to feed themselves there, they constantly raided American settlements along the border. This forced the United States government to offer the Mexican Kickapoo a reservation in Oklahoma and after successful negotiations some settled there in 1873–1874. The remaining populations live in Kansas, Oklahoma, and Chihuahua, Mexico.

238

Mahican or Mohican

The Mahican Confederacy, of the Eastern Woodlands culture, consisted of several groups, one of which was the Mohegan. The similarity of names often leads to confusion, especially as both groups are sometimes called Mohicans. The Mohegan tribe was the eastern branch of the Mahican Confederacy. In the early 1600s they inhabited lands that covered most of southwest Connecticut. At this time the Mohegan did not exist as a separate group; they were part of the Pequot tribe whose name means "destroyers." The two tribes split after a rebellion by an internal faction, by what became the Mohegan, against an unpopular chief called Sassacus. He was finally deposed when the Pequot killed an English trader. The British retaliated and roughly 500 members of the tribe were killed in the ensuing battles. The survivors escaped in various directions, with one group led by Sassacus being captured and killed or sold as slaves by the Mohawk. Those who were not caught settled where they could among the other tribes of southern New England. The rest of the Mahican Confederacy fared little better. The Mohawk used guns provided by the Dutch to defeat and disperse them. A few Mahican still survive, with most of them living in Connecticut and Wisconsin.

The Menominee (also spelled Menomini) were people who had a gatherer culture. Their main foodstuff was wild rice which they gathered in large quantities. Their name comes from the word *manomin*, which is Algonquian for "wild rice." In the 1630s they inhabited the fertile lands at the mouth of the Menominee River in Wisconsin and Michigan. Although they had peaceful relations with the white settlers, they fought bitter wars with many of the other local tribes who wanted to seize the places where the wild rice grew so successfully. They managed to hold on to these homelands until 1854 when they were moved to the Menominee Reservation on the Wolf River in northcentral Wisconsin. The tribe became independent of Federal Control in 1961.

MICMAC

The Micmac (also spelled Mi'kmaq, Mikmaq, or Mikmak) inhabits lands across Nova Scotia, Cape Breton Island, Prince Edward Island, Newfoundland, and New Brunswick in Canada. Because their lands were surrounded by water they became very skilled canoeists and obtained most of their foodstuffs from fishing or hunting from boats. The first consistent contact they had with Europeans was with French missionaries in the early 1600s. As a result they became allied to the French; indeed, their name translates as "allies." They did not suffer the usual tribulations that most of the other native peoples endured, and the tribe is still flourishing, albeit in a very different form. These days, the tribe earn most of their income from farming.

The Mohawk have had a turbulent history in the years since the Europeans arrived on the continent. The name was given to them by the Algonquin Nation and translates as "they who eat animate things" or "man-eaters." They called themselves Kaniengehaga or Kanien'kehaka, which means "people of the place of the flint." They were the most easterly of tribes of the Iroquois Confederacy and during the warmer parts of the year they lived along the St. Lawrence River. When it got colder, they moved to the Mohawk Valley in central New York state where they had permanent long houses. These could be up to 120-feet long and were covered in tree bark. The Mohawk had three clans: the Bear, Wolf, and Turtle clans. The Mohawk were a warlike people who fought most of the other tribes in the region. These wars affected their population so badly that by the end of the 15th century they almost completely disappeared. When the Dutch gave them guns to help hunt beaver, they also used them to good effect to defeat their enemies. The Mohawk had a ritual of cooking and eating their prisoners. The common people were allowed to eat the limbs and torso, but the chiefs ate the heart and the head. The tribe fought for the British in the Revolutionary War and afterward were given lands in Canada by the British government. The Mohawk peoples who remained in the United States were driven out by the Oneida in 1777. Most of the surviving members still live in Canada.

The Ojibwa and the Chippewa are the same tribe. These are not different names, but different spellings of the same word, causing much confusion because of the unusual native pronunciation. Ojibwa can also be spelled Ojibway, Ojibwe, and Ojibwemowin. The Northern Ojibwa formerly inhabited lands on the shores of Lake Superior, Wisconsin. Here they were a hunter-gatherer peoples, who grew corn and squash, collected wild rice, and hunted deer or fished the rivers and lakes. The rich source of wild rice on their lands was envied by both the Sioux and the Fox, and as a result, the Ojibwa were in a more or less permanent state of war with them. Fortunately, they managed to get hold of guns before their enemies did, and around 1690 they forced the Fox out of the region. Shortly after this they expelled the Sioux and expanded their territories as far afield as central North Dakota. The Ojibwa who moved to this new area became known as the Plains Ojibwa. They also obtained large tracts of land from the Iroquois after defeating them, which meant that by the mid-1700s they became one of the largest tribes in North America. At this time their population was around 25,000. The tribe signed a treaty with the United States government in 1812, and since they have lived on reservations in Michigan, Wisconsin, Minnesota, and North Dakota. Today around 50,000 Ojibwa are living on reservations in Canada.

YAHA-HAJO.
A SEMINOLE CHIEF.

The Oneida are an ancient people who formerly inhabited lands between the St. Lawrence River and the Pennsylvania border. They were one of the tribes that made up the Iroquois Confederacy, and were, like the Mohawk, divided into three clans - the Bear, Wolf and Turtle Clans. They were farmers who would also hunt buffalo and other game animals when the opportunity was there. When the European settlers arrived, the Iroquois were quick to exploit the chance to obtain modern items - especially the gun, by trading beaver furs with them. In the Revolutionary War the other members of the Iroquois Confederacy had fought for the British. The Oneida, however, had sided with the Americans, and although they were on the winning side they were expelled from their lands. The United States government gave them a treaty to protect their lands in New York, but as was usual back then, the deals were duplicitous, and their 6 million acres were soon reduced to almost nothing. Many members of the tribe moved away to Canada and Wisconsin in the 1830s, however, a few decided to remain. Ever since then, they have tried to get legal recompense for having their ancestral lands taken from them - the affair is ongoing, and will undoubtedly continue for some time yet.

OTTAWA

The Ottawa tribe formerly inhabited lands across the southern part of Michigan in the area of the Grand River, as well as in Ohio and Indiana. The tribe's name comes from the Algonquian word *adawe*, which means "to trade," referring to their practice of buying and selling items across a wide area. They had especially good trade connections with both the Ojibwa and the Potawatomi. In the mid-1600s the tribe was forced to move west to the Green Bay, Wisconsin, area due to the onset of wars. By 1700 they had spread all over the region, from southern Wisconsin to northern Illinois, to Lake Huron, to Lake Erie, and from Detroit eastward to Pennsylvania. The Ottawa had a powerful chief called Pontiac who was determined to stop the British taking all their lands. In 1763 he started a war, but was not successful in getting all the other native tribes to join with him. Realizing he could not win, he finally made peace in 1765. The tribe were forced to hand over their lands in Ohio in 1831. Although they were given new territories in Kansas, these were soon taken from them, and they were allotted land in the Indian Territories in Oklahoma instead, where their descendants still remain.

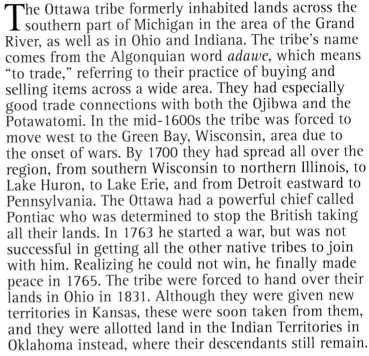

PEQUOT

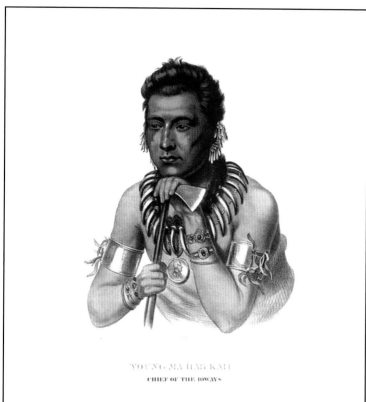

YOUNG MA HAS KAH
CHIEF OF THE IOWAYS

Once resident in Connecticut, the Pequot were decimated in 1637 by a force composed of the English and of two Indian tribes—the Mohegan and Narragansett. Few were left after the captives were sold into West Indian slavery, and those that remain today live near Ledyard. They are one of the few groups that can claim ancestry back to the original inhabitants of southern New England.

SAULTEAUX OR NORTHERN OJIBWA

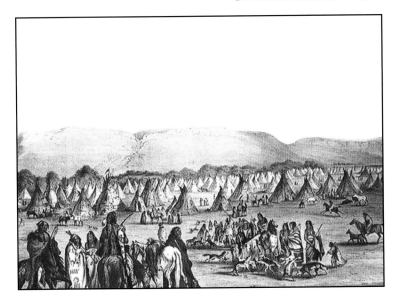

Originally living in the Eastern Woodlands, the Saulteaux or Northern Ojibwa moved northwest both because of European population pressure and also the lucrative fur trade. A sizeable tribe (over 30,000 were reported in 1978), those that are left are difficult to differentiate from other Ojibwan and Cree peoples.

KEOKUK
CHIEF OF THE SACS & FOXES

PUBLISHED BY F. W. GREENOUGH, PHILAD.ᵃ

The Sauk, or Sac, tribe is closely related to the Fox, but the two are separate tribes which in 1600 occupied the eastern half of lower Michigan between Saginaw Bay and Detroit. Both of their oral histories tell of an earlier time when they migrated from the Atlantic coast via the St. Lawrence River. When this happened is unclear. The Sauk lived around Saginaw Bay, which is named from them, whereas the Fox were just to the south and west. Driven from their homeland during the 1640s, the Fox resettled in central Wisconsin. The Sauk crossed over to the upper peninsula near the Mackinac Strait and moved into the headwaters of the Wisconsin River west of Green Bay. Except for the two years of 1710 to 1712, when the Fox lived near Detroit, Michigan, neither tribe ever returned to that area. They remained in Wisconsin until 1734, when both were driven across the Mississippi River into eastern Iowa by the French.

SHAWNEE

The Shawnee tribe formerly inhabited lands in Ohio, although by the mid-1600s the tribe had split in two with one part living in western South Carolina and the other in northern Tennessee. They continued to move around separately for about 100 years, until they joined up again in the mid-18th century in Ohio; at this stage the tribe's population was around 1,500. They were a warlike tribe who took part in most of the wars in the northwest region. In 1795, a treaty forced them to give up their territories in Ohio and relocate to Indiana. They tried staging an uprising at the beginning of the 19th century, but this failed and they were once again forced to move, first, to Missouri, then to Kansas, and finally in Oklahoma. Today about 2,250 Shawnee still live on reservations in Oklahoma.

INDEX